basic atonal COUNTERPOINT

STANLEY a. fUNICELLI

CONTENTS

preface

PART 1 single-line construction   1
chapter 1 set procedures   1
    general considerations   1
    the vector and transposition   5
    the set list   7
    subsets and supersets   7

chapter 2 guidelines   8
    pitch use   8
    rhythm, meter, and articulation   9

chapter 3 the first phrase   12
    pitch generation and controlling factors   12
    analysis   13
    shape and climax   15
    registral use   17
    rhythm   17
    the revised phrase   18

chapter 4 the phrase group   21
    fragment transformation   21
    expanded intervallic usage   23

chapter 5 the embellished line   26
    basic procedures   26
    the nested pitch field   28

chapter 6 transformations and variants   33
    inversional, registral, and intervallic exchange   33
    dissonance/consonant exchange   34
    refinements of contour   35
    traditional variants   36

chapter 7 Intersection   37
   re-ordered partitions   39

chapter 8 episodic variations   42
   instrumental considerations   42
   the compositional plan   43
   form and structure   44
   rhythmic variation   46

PART 2 multivoice composition
chapter 9 two-voice writing   51
   general principles   51
   models of two-voice procedures: 1 vs. 4   52
   shaping the second voice   56
   1 vs. 2   57
   held or repeated tone   59
   note-against-note   60
   second line climax   63

chapter 10 refinements of the two-voice model   65
   cartwheel motion   65
   anticipation and suspension   66
   interpolation   66
   imitation   67

chapter 11 the nature and use of dissonance   72
   the basis of perception   73
   intervallic order   74
   dissonance factors   75
   df: inherent and by spacing   75
   comparison and projected factors   76
   application   77

chapter 12 multi-voice settings   84
   recurrent set use   84
   use of multiple sets   85
   refinements   86
   generating a fourth voice   87

chapter 13 fantasia for string quartet   93

PART 3 on-going variation: free counterpoint   101
chapter 14 dyadic Generation   101

chapter 15 motivic usage   108
     motivic extraction   108
     set association   109
     expanded motivic usage   111
     derivation of the motive   112
     analysis   116
     compositional considerations   126

afterward   127

preface

The goal of the present study is the creation of aural comprehension in atonal composition through the use of counterpoint.

Atonal composition is a relatively recent development. Most of the materials available that describe or analyze atonal procedures are rather narrow and deal in great detail with rather complex issues. In fact, many writers in this field tend, unfortunately, to equate complexity with profundity, and to rely on ever more obscure formulations that are further and further removed from music and music-making. Also, many such writings only present specific devices and little or no information on the most pertinent aspect of atonal composition – pitch choice.*

This volume will present an ordered approach to beginning composition with atonal materials. It will explore pitch choice and the contrapuntal framework. It will present procedures for the construction, development and presentation of cogent musical thought. Form and structure will also be addressed and will be seen to grow out of local-level procedures into the formulation of a complete work. And most importantly this volume aims at fostering the ability to think musically in the atonal world.

*An indispensable volume is *The Structure of Atonal Music* by Allen Forte, the seminal work in the field: an excellent tool for understanding set-related procedures demonstrated through insightful analyses of 20th Century works.

part 1
single-line construction

chapter 1

SET PROCEDURES

general considerations

Atonal music is based primarily on intervallic considerations. Even in passages of very dense texture or in works that purport to rely entirely on strict or free twelve-tone procedures, close study will often reveal a predilection for certain intervals or groups of intervals. Far from being a mere surface-level occurrence, such recognizable and recurrent use reflects a choice. As atonal possibilities far exceed those of tonal styles, such choices reveal something of the local-level or large scale procedures and, therefor, the compositional intent of the composer.

A language has evolved over the past several decades which can describe atonal compositions in great detail, including the identification of materials, compositional procedures and their application. This language is known as set theory.

Sets are expressed as numbers. Set procedures rely on simple manipulations of numbers. The use of sets does not mean that we must distance ourselves from notes any more than the use of notes on the staff distances us from sound (although there are many who do not "hear" what they write but produce "paper music" – dots on paper or groups of numbers). Atonal music is intervalically generated. Intervals are a measure of distance. The use of numbers in sets allows us to accurately measure the distances between groups of intervals and to conceive of relationships which include a diversity of materials.

The alternative to the use of sets is the narrative approach, still favored by some writers. It is unwieldy, imprecise, and often confuses local stylistic usage with identity.

For instance, let us examine the group of pitches CFG. This has been described as being a 4th and 5th above C or a 2nd and 5th above F, as a chord built of 4ths -GCF – or of 5ths – FCG. Attempts have been made to explain its occurrence in terms of its similarity to tonal constructions; as a C Major triad "clouded" by the inclusion of a 4th instead of a 3rd, or a F Major clouded by a 2nd; or as a C or F Major sonority with a "false bass" (F)CG or (G)FC.

All tell us something about the collection – namely the styles in which they were employed, their appearance or local usage. Regardless of style, all are simply forms of set 027. All other explanations relate to specific instances which emphasize stylistic differences. By focusing instead on similarities we have the ability to demonstrably contrast widely divergent styles.

(The following represents a very abbreviated account of set terminology and procedures and is not intended as more than a mere cursory introduction. Clarification and expansion of concepts occur throughout the body of the text.)

pitch and interval notation

The pitches C-B are represented by the integers 0-11, known as pitch classes (pc's).

C	C#/Db	D	D#/Eb	E	F	F#/Gb	G	G#/Ab	A	A#/Bb	B
0	1	2	3	4	5	6	7	8	9	10	11

Further, all octaves of any given pitch are said to be members of that pitch class. All Cs belong to pc0, all C#s and Dbs belong to pc1, etc. This allows us to disregard registral placement of tones if we so choose and to perceive of all octave duplications as being essentially the same pitch. This is known as octave equivalence.

Just as all pitches are represented by numbers, so are intervals. Only six prime intervals exist, all others being either inversions or compounds of the six. The distance of an interval is expressed as the number of half-steps spanned. These distances are called interval classes (ic's).

ic(prime)	inversion	compound
1(m2)	11(M7)	13(m9)ic1+12
2(M2)	10(m7)	14(M9)ic2+12
3(m3)	9(M6)	15(m10)
4(M3)	8(m6)	16(M10)
5(P4)	7(P5)	. 17(P11)
6(A4)	6(d5)	18(A11)

Notice that an ic and its inversion add to 12, the number of half steps in the octave, while tonal intervals and their inversions equal 9 – one more than the octave. With tonal intervals one tone is counted twice – as the upper tone of one interval and the bottom of its inversion;

$$
\begin{array}{ll}
6 & C \\
3 \quad E \quad 1 & E \text{ (counted twice)} \\
1 \, C &
\end{array}
$$

Ic's measure the distance above a pitch, not including that pitch (e.g. A/Bb = ic1 not m2). Notice also that compound intervals add 12, the half-steps contained in the octave, to the ic; 13(m9) = ic1 + ic12.

To find a specific ic, merely subtract the pc of the lower-occurring tone from the higher. Therefore, pc's 0/2, 3/5 and 9/11 are all members of ic2. If the lower tone is, say, pc11 and the upper is pc3, add twelve to the upper tone before subtracting to yield ic4. This is a fairly simple procedure relying on octave equivalence and can be proved as being an inversion of pc's 3 and 11 = ic8, whose inversion is ic4.

No distinction is made in the case of enharmonic spellings: C# and Db are considered identical members of pc1. Thus, C#/A#, C#/Bb, Db/A# and Db/Bb are all pc's 1/10 = ic9.

Assn.1: Assign pc's and calculate ic's for the intervals below. Show actual and prime intervals where appropriate.

sets:normal and inversional order

A set consists of three or more pitches. The members of the set may occur in any order or register, much as the members of a major triad may be distributed in any order or register and still retain their identity as a major triad.

Consider the following 4-member (4n) sets.

To find the set, first convert the pitches to pc's as shown. Next, we must find the normal order. This means that the pc's are arranged so that they cover the smallest possible distance from first to last, containing the smallest possible ic's. To accomplish this, first place the pc's in ascending order from low to high. Calculate the ic's from the first pc to all following.

$$
\begin{array}{llll}
\text{pc's} & 1\ 2\ 5\ 7 & 3\ 7\ 8\ 11 & 2\ 4\ 10\ 11 & 1\ 7\ 8\ 11 \\
\text{ic's} & 1\ 4\ 6 & 4\ 5\ 8 & 2\ 8\ 9 & 6\ 7\ 10
\end{array}
$$

To be sure we have the smallest possible span, subject the collection to circular permutation by repositioning the first pc as the last. Repeat the process until all pc's have been placed in the first position. That ordering of the pc's which spans the smallest distance with the smallest ic's to the left is the normal order.

$$
\begin{array}{llll}
\text{e.g.} & 1\ 2\ 5\ 7 & 2\ 5\ 7\ 1 & 5\ 7\ 1\ 2 & 7\ 1\ 2\ 5 \\
& 1\ 4\ 6 & 3\ 5\ 11 & 2\ 8\ 9 & 6\ 7\ 10
\end{array}
$$

Assn. 2: Calculate the normal order for the remaining 4n sets shown above.

Now the normal order must be converted to prime form. This allows us to compare sets of similar, dissimilar or identical construction or size. To accomplish this, the pc's must be transposed by some ic (T-level = level of transposition) so that the set begins on 0: simply subtract the first integer from all integers, effecting a transposition of all set members by the same distance. This is the set in prime form.

$$
\begin{array}{cccc}
1 & 2 & 5 & 7 \\
\underline{-1} & \underline{-1} & \underline{-1} & \underline{-1} \\
=0 & 1 & 4 & 6
\end{array}
$$

Assn. 3: Find the prime form of the remaining sets.

Consider the following collection of pitches.

$$
\begin{array}{llll}
\text{pc's} & 2\ 3\ 9\ 11 & 3\ 9\ 11\ 2 & 9\ 11\ 2\ 3 & 11\ 2\ 3\ 9 \\
\text{ic's} & 1\ 7\ 9 & 6\ 8\ 11 & 2\ 5\ 6 & 3\ 4\ 10
\end{array}
$$

The order 9,11,2,3 spans the smallest distance but the smallest ic is to the right. This is an inversional form of the set. If read from right to left – that is, calculate the distances below the last pc – the distances become:

$$9\ 11\ 2\ 3$$
$$6\ \ 4\ 1.$$

To find the prime form, exchange the position of the pc's so that the last occurs first and the first occurs last (descending order). Add the newly positioned first pc to itself. Now find some integer which when added to each succeeding pc will produce the same sum. Those integers which were employed to result in the identical sum are the normal order. The prime form may now be found as explained above.

$$9\ \ 11\ \ 2\ \ 3\ \ \text{becomes}\ \ 3\ \ 2\ \ 11\ \ 9$$

$$
\begin{array}{cccc}
3 & 2 & 11 & 9 \\
+3 & +4 & +7 & +9 \\
\hline
=6 & 6 & 18 & 18
\end{array}
$$

$$
\begin{array}{cccc}
3 & 4 & 7 & 9 \\
-3 & -3 & -3 & -3 \\
\hline
=0 & 1 & 4 & 6
\end{array}
$$

Assn. 4: Find the normal order and prime form of the following sets.

the vector and transposition

The set displays total pitch content but not total intervallic content. This is the function of the six-place ordered array known as the vector. Each of the six positions of the vector represents one of the six prime ic's. All oc-currences of ic1 are shown in the first position, all ic's 2 in the second position, etc. If no instance of a specific ic occurs in the set the vector contains a 0 in that position.

To calculate the vector, first determine the ic's which are formed from the first pc to all following pc's. Repeat the process from the second pc to all following, etc.

for set 0,1,3,4,7	ic1	ic2	ic3	ic4	ic5	ic6
	0/1		0/3	0/4	0/7	
		1/3	1/4			1/7
	3/4			3/7		
		4/7				
	2	1	3	2	1	1

Notice that a 5n set contains 10 intervals. Four are formed with the first pc, three with the second, two with the third and one with the fourth: $4+3+2+1=10$. A 4n set contains $3+2+1=6$ intervals. This is expressed as 5n! or 4n! and is read as "five factorial".

The vector allows for comparison of sets of dissimilar construction and size. All sets have a distinct vector except for those sets which include an internal -Z. These sets constitute a special case in that they share an identical vector with a set of dissimilar construction. Two such sets are called Z-related pairs.

4-Z15 0,1,4,6 [111111]   4-Z 29 0,1,3,7 [111111]

The vector is of great value in choosing T-levels, informing you at a glance as to how many tones remain invariant, or recur, at any level of transposition. For instance, the vector of 0,2,3,7 is [111120]. The positions for ic's 1,2,3,4 all show one entry. There are two entries for ic1 and none for ic6. This means that transposition by T1, T2, T3, T4 will all result in one invariant pc, two invariant pc's at T5 and none at T6. This is true whether at T+1 or T-1.

T-1;	11 1 2 6	T-2; 10 0 1 5	T-3; 9 11 0 4
T0;	0 2 3 7	0 2 3 7	0 2 3 7
T+1;	1 3 4 8	T+2; 2 4 5 9	T+3; 3 5 6 10
T-4;	8 10 11 3	T-5; 7 9 10 2	T-6; 6 8 9 1
	0 2 3 7	0 2 3 7	0 2 3 7
T+4;	4 6 7 11	T+5; 5 7 8 0	T+6; 6 8 9 1

Notice that transposition by a T-level of +/-6 are identical, as the tritone is its own inversion.

the set list

The set list provided as an appendix is an invaluable tool. First of all, sets of identical size are listed in order of total span, from narrowest to widest intervals. To the left is the name of the set followed by the sets content, vector and its complement, also showing name, contents and vector.

If we employ the tones of some 3n set, nine pitches of the total chromatic have not been used. These comprise the complement to the 3n set. Complements are shown for all 3,4,5n sets (the 9,8,7n sets, respectively). Many 6n sets show no complement; they are their own complement.

subsets and supersets

As you may have already realized, sets of larger numbers of members contain a number of smaller sets. The smaller sets are called subsets, the larger supersets.

   0,1,6 [100011]   0,1,5,7 [110121]   0,1,4,7 [102111]   0,1,4,5,7 [212221]

The vectors for the sets listed above all contain ic's 1,5,6. All show 0,1 as the first set members, while the last three show 0,1,7. 0,1,5,7 and 0,1,4,7 are contained in 0,1,4,5,7. All contain 016 (017). We may say that the 4n and 5n sets are supersets of 016; that is, all contain 016 and something else. The 3n and 4n sets are subsets of the 5n set.

Some supersets contain pitches all of which are involved in at least one form of some particular subset. Such supersets are said to maximize that particular subset. If only one version of a subset appears in a certain superset, the subset may be said to be minimally represented.

Assn. 5: Extract all possible subsets from the following supersets. Check to be sure your extracted subset is in normal order. Reduce the subsets to prime form. Calculate the vectors for the super- and subsets. Find the set names on the set list.

   0,2,3,7   0,1,2,6,8   0,2,3,4,6,9

chapter 2

GUIDELINES

Pitches are generated by some procedure, abstract or concrete, defined with great precision or in only the most general terms. The use of a motive is the most concrete procedure with all parameters defined: specific pitches in specific order combining to form a succession of specific intervals which are collected in specific sets; the pitches are supported by specific rhythm and specific registers. The articulation and dynamic's associated with the occurrence of the motive may also be factors considered as intrinsic to the appearance and generative procedures of the motive.

The most general or abstract definitions can be as vague as "rhythm: long-short" or "intervals: narrow-wide", etc. Such general guidelines are of value only if they are strongly informed and refined by pitch-oriented approaches. Therefore, we will concern ourselves wholly with procedures which focus on the orderly, associative generation of pitch and will consider all other parameters governing musical composition and performance to be in service to the comprehension of orderly progress on the level of pitch.

Atonal lines tend to avoid fragments which suggest tonal use. As we progress further in this study, you will become more sensitive to the appearance of such groups on the level of note-to-note or between tones associated by their placement in similar registers or by stress.

Generative or governing procedures which are well defined, at least in regard to some parameter, will help guide pitch choice and registral placement. The logical unfolding of these procedures will be undertaken in a manner to focus the ear strongly toward the process and its goal.

pitch use

Any number of tones may be used in the line. However, too few notes tend to be heard as isolated gestures. Large groups of tones will generally be seen to be comprised of two or more smaller groupings, fragments or sub-phrases.

There is no specific need to avoid jumps or adhere primarily to step-wise motion. Lines or fragments may consist primarily of jumps or steps, although most lines will exhibit a balanced mixture of both as the logic of the piece demands. Their interaction will serve to provide contour to the generation of pitches. The resultant lines will exhibit shapes or gestures which may serve to focus the set on various registral levels while providing graceful, well-placed climaxes. Jumps may be employed to guide the ear toward unfoldings of the governing procedures over longer time spans.

Pitches may be repeated with care. They may occur as simple rhythmic repetitions. The same tone may occur as the last tone of one fragment and as the first tone of the next in order to heighten a real or perceived association. A tone may occur as the first and last tone of a fragment, prolonged by intervening tones. This will often effect closure of greater or lesser strength, depending on other factors. Such use of a boundary tone should be employed only when closure is intended and/or can be featured as a facet of the overall design.

A group of fragments may all begin from a given pitch (invariant). This is generally employed to prolong the importance of that tone over some time span and/or to signal a similarity relationship among the fragments.

A group of fragments may include a repeated tone placed in various positions. In example 3, below, all recurrences of pc11 occur at pitch. Octave repetitions are generally not used, although in very dense textures they can hardly be avoided. Whether at pitch or at the octave, repeated tones are generally presented in different context. The closer the repeat the more the appearance of the tone, its function and surroundings should be varied.

rhythm, meter, and articulation

Articulation and rhythm are employed to further refine the presentation of the chosen materials and design. Atonal composition tends to feature non-regular rhythmic units and values. Once a specific rhythm or group of values has been presented, it tends to wish to assert itself throughout the composition in varied, related or recurrent form.

An excellent procedure for avoiding the "tyranny of the barline" is to dispense with them entirely at first, notating the length of sound or silence with no regard for meter. Barlines should then be added to the rhythmic line, re-notating the rhythm as necessary to agree with the chosen meter.

In choosing meter, two very different procedures may be followed. The first, much favored by inexperienced composers, is to provide a constantly

changing meter which supposedly assures a varied rhythmic character. The meters are chosen to reflect the rhythm and articulation of the
phrase or collection of pitches.

While some sections of a composition may, indeed, necessitate such a
fluctuation of meters, there are two pitfalls. First, a scheme of changing
meters assures nothing but that the performer will encounter difficulties
in getting a rhythmic "feel" for a passage, and the composer may be lulled
into thinking he has provided rhythmic variety because of the complex
appearance of the line. In fact, it is possible to fall into a regular recurrence of rhythm regardless of the complexity of metric change. The other
drawback is that a changing meter employed to agree with the phrasing of
the line becomes a meaningless exercise when conflicting rhythmic units
occur in a multi-voice composition. One must decide which of the conflicting rhythmic units should be given primacy in deciding metric choice.
The conflicts arising from the disagreement among simultaneously occurring rhythms and non-recurrent meter often present insurmountable
problems in ensemble.

Rhythm and meter, like all other factors, are in service to the orderly
presentation of the work. They must convey the composers's intentions to
the performer. In a single-line work, it is possible to employ bar-lines to
signal the end of a succession of pitches intended to be heard as a group.
In such a case, no meter need be noted, allowing the performer to react to
length of sound or silence and not their placement within the bar-line.

A regular meter may be featured so that the performer will have a
constantly recurring metric unit against which to judge the rhythmic
appearance of the line. Here, articulation and phrasing will be employed
to counteract the bar-line and shape the values of the regular meter into
the intended irregular rhythmic groupings. This is the most useful procedure in multi-voice writing, especially of a complex or conflicting over-all
rhythmic texture, often greatly reducing problems of ensemble.

Another procedure of the inexperienced composer is to provide a constant fluctuation of irregular subdivisions of the beat or governing rhythmic
value quintuplets, septuplets, et al and often occurring in close succession
in irregular meter against other conflicting subdivisions. Rhythm, as previously stated, tends to assert itself throughout a piece. A reliance on a varied
use of odd subdivisions becomes unwieldy and results in an imprecise and
muddy texture even after hours of rehearsal. A good rule of thumb is to
write only those rhythms and horizontal or vertical combinations that you

can hear, feel and perform, and then only if they clearly convey the sense of your materials.

When a very complex rhythmic texture is a necessity to your overall design, you may wish to employ proportional notation. Here, no normal rhythmic values are used, the duration of a tone being represented by the visual distance by which it is separated from preceding and succeeding pitches. This has several advantages. It allows for very dense groupings of tones within one "beat" without asking the performer to accurately perform complex subdivisions with rhythmic precision. It allows the performer more spontaneity and gives a less forbidding appearance to your score.

There are various appearances to proportional notation, but the following usage may prove most useful. Use stems only to the first and last notes of an articulated phrase or phrase group. Ligatures and other such devices may be used to further refine the articulation of the phrase. Use beams between these stems to indicate the compositional/structural unit.

In ensemble pieces bar-lines may be used as well as either shorter vertical lines across the staff or slashes above to indicate the placement of the regular rhythmic unit. This has the added value of being more flexible than strict proportional notation, as a longer rhythmic unit with little activity may be written in a compressed area, and a shorter complex unit may be given more room on the page. These notational devices may be employed in alternation or in vertical combination with normal rhythmic notation.

EX.4

chapter 3

THE FIRST PHRASE

<u>pitch generation and controlling factors</u>

Some decisions are necessary before we begin to compose. First, let us choose to employ all twelve tones with no repeats within the line. As literally thousands of lines could be written to fulfill this stricture, it is necessary to choose some controlling or governing factor in order to provide our line with aural coherence. A controlling set (or group of sets) is of great value in providing unity, variety and focus to the unfolding of the line and a structural design. Let us choose a 3n set, 3-2 (0,1,3 and its inversion 0,2,3), and feature strong links between successive appearances of the set.

The opening statement of the line could be ordered to expose either the step-wise ic's 1 and 2, or to feature one step-wise ic and ic3(9). The latter possibility will allow for greater diversity due to its varied surface of step and skip. Let the opening pc's be 11,0,9 – BCA. The last two pc's of our opening form ic3. The opening pitch combines with ic3 to present 3-2 in inversion.

Pc10 can be used to generate the next form of 3-2. Pc10 can exist as any member of the normal or inversional form of the set, as shown below.

Bb=O	Bb,B,C#	Bb,C,C#
Bb=1	A,Bb,C	
Bb=2	Ab,Bb,B	
Bb=3	G,Ab,Bb	G,A,Bb

Only the collection G,Ab,Bb, provides all new tones. When placed in order Bb,Ab,G one new interval is exposed, ic2, with ic-1 employed to balance the two apparent versions of ic+1 in the opening four notes, B,C and A,Bb. (Read ic-1 as down by the interval of 1, ic+1 as up by ic1). The last two pc's of this grouping will again generate a linking version. Only pc5 – F – can perform this function.

At this point, we have exposed seven of the total twelve pitches we have decided to employ in our line. Only pc's 1,2,3,6 – C#,D,D#,F# – have not been used. We can confine our search for our new version of the set to these tones.

Our linking pc5 can combine with the four remaining pc's to form several versions of 3-2; C#,D,E, C#,D#,E, D#,E,F#. If we choose C#,D# we are left with D and F# for our last set. As these form an ic not found in 3-2, they will not be employed together. If we use C#,D,E, the remaining pc's 3,6 must be completed by pc's 4 or 5, both of which have already been used. If we follow E with F# and D#, the remaining C# and D could complete set 3-2 with either E or B. Whatever our choice we can form no linking version of the set ending on F.

Let C# and D be placed as members of the last set. Either E or B will serve to act as boundaries, B to the entire line, E to the last six pc's. Such boundaries affect a feeling of closure, as previously noted.

Ending on E will effectively isolate the end of the line, suggesting that the strong links exhibited in the opening of the line are intentionally dissolved at the end. This would suggest a process. We could further heighten this feeling of a process at work if the ending six pc's are placed in order (B,C,A,Bb,Ab G,F)E,F#,D#,C#,D,E, as this order presents two successive collections each reducible to set 4-1; G,F,E,F# and D#,C#,D,E. If B were placed in the last position no such relationship would surface and apparent isolation of the last three unlinked tones would be heightened. These tones would be forced to act as a coda or as the beginning of a new phrase.

analysis

An examination of the ic's and 3n-6n sets formed by the line may reveal further relationships to be exploited.

pc's	B	C	A	Bb	Ab	G	F	E	F#	D#	C#	D	E
ic's	+1	-3	+1	-2		-1	-2	-1	+2	-3	-2	+1	+2

3n	11,0,9		0,9 10		9,10,8		10,8,7	8,7,5		7,5,4		
	0,1,3I		0,1,3		0,1,2		0,1,3	0,1,3I		0,1,3		

	5,4,6		4,6,3		6,3,1		3,1,2	1,2 11 or 1,2,4		
	0,1,2		0,1,3		0,2,5		0,1,2	0,1,3I	0,1,3	

4n	11,0,9,10	0,9,10,8	9,10,8,7	10,8,7,5	8,7,5,4	7,5,4,6
	0,1,2,3	0,1,2,4	0,1,2,3	0,2,3,5	0,1,3,4	0,1,2,3

	5,4,6,3	4,6,3,1	6,3,1,2	3,1,2,11 or 3,1,2,4	
	0,1,2,3	0,23,5	0,1,2,5	0,1,2,4I	0,1,2,3

5n	11,0,9,10,8	0,9,10,8,7	9,10,8,7,5	10,8,7,5,4	8,7,5,4,6
	0,1,2,3,4	0,1,2,3,5	0,1,2,3,5I	0,1,3,4,6	0,1,2,3,4

	7,5,4,6,3	5,4,6,3,1	4,6,3,1,2	6,3,1,2,11 or 6,3,1,2,4	
	0,1,2,3,4	0,1,2,3,5I	0,1,2,3,5	0,2,3,4,7	0,1,2,3,5

6n	11,0,9,10,8,7	0,9,10,8,7,5	9,10,8,7,5,4	10,8,7,5,4,6
	0,1,2,3,4,5	0,2,3,4,5,7	0,1,2,3,5,6I	0,1,2,3,4,6

	8,7,5,4,6,3	7,5,4,6,3,1	5,4,6,3,1,2	4,6,3,1,2,11 or (4,6,3,1,2,4)	
	0,1,2,3,4,5	0,1,2,3,4,6I	0,1,2,3,4,5	0,2,3,4,5,7	0,1,2,3,5

Notice first the ic's formed by our line. There are five occurrences of ic1, four of ic2 and three of ic3. The first half of the line exhibits recurrent ic1 separated by other ic's from our set. The second half shows a palindrome of ic's of increasing/decreasing size around the central ic3. This occurs at the end of the linked forms of 3-2.

The 3n sets show a preponderance of set 3-2 with three occurrences of 3-1 and one of 3-7 (0,2,5). This latter set, while having ic's 2 and 3 in common with 3-2 is very different in "sound" from any surrounding trichord, due to its vector. This set occurs at the point of procedural disparity in our line.

The 4n sets include four appearances of 4-1 (0,1,2,3), five if pc4 ends the line, two of 0,2,3,5 and one each of 0,1,2,5, 0,1,3,4, and 0,1,2,4 (two if pc11 is used). The succession of these sets is rather more graceful than that of the 3n sets, which feature 3-2 as per our design, with one greatly dissimilar set. If associated in 4n groups, a closely related series of sets is exposed, featuring minimal intervallic difference.

0,1,2,3 0,1,3,4 0,1,2,5 0,1,2,4I or 0,1,2,3

If sets are articulated excluding the opening pc, a graceful succession is still achieved.

0,1,2,4 0,1,2,3 0,1,2,4 or 0,1,2,3

On the 5n level the following sets exist: 0,1,2,3,5 (4 or 5), 0,1,2,3,4, (3), 0,1,2,3,6 and 0,2,3,4,7. The last two anomalous sets are easy to avoid, allowing us to focus on sets which could account for the entire line. To avoid 0,1,3,4,6 simply avoid articulation which would include the tones of that set. Ending on B would result in 0,2,3,4,7; ending on E yields 0,1,2,3,5. This suggests that if we choose to articulate a surface of 5n sets we might best employ pc4 at the end of our line.

Appearances of 0,1,2,3,4,5 dominate the 6n level with three occurrences, followed by two occurrences each of 0,2,3,4,5,7 and 0,1,2,3,4,6. There is one occurrence of 0,1,2,3,5,6. Surface articulation of 6n could result in a strong relationship between first and second halves of the line, as set 6-1(0,1,2,3,4,5) exists as the first and last six tones if pc4 is used to end the line. Care must be exercised in setting pc5, mid-way in the line, as this tone must be heard in association with the last tone of the first 6n set for purposes of articulation of sub-phrases, but is a member of the last 6n set, as well.

	B	C	A	Bb	Ab	G	F	E	F#	D#	C#	D	E
4n	9,10,11,0				4,5,7,8				1,2,3,6				
			7,8,9,10				3,4,5,6		1,2,3,4				
5n		7,8,9,10,0					1,3,4,5,6						
			5,7,8,9,1 0					1,2,3,4,6					
6n	7,8,9,10,11,0					1,2,3,4,5,6							

shape and climax

If the pitches of the line were to be placed in closest proximity the entire sweep of the line would be downward, a possibility but one which shows no grace or imagination, no climax and, due to the similarity of successive ic's, no variety or feeling of progression. Surface articulation of 4n-6n sets may mitigate this somewhat, although the lack of climax is a serious fault, but one which is fairly simple to remedy: we simply need to invert some interval of the original line.

A single upward jump would appear as an anomaly in the line, both by virtue of its isolated existence in an upper register and the single occurrence of a rather wide interval. Both factors impress the ear strongly as we tend to hear anomalies, especially of this type, as differentiated from the general progress of the line on some level. It is best to place several pitches in this upper register, as preparatory and/or subsequent tones to the actual climax of the line, and to associate them in some manner that reveals something of the inner working of the line, now over a longer span of time.

We may logically choose to feature our governing set in the upper register. To accomplish this, we must examine the line for non-contiguous occurrences of set 3-2.

B C A Bb Ab G F E F# D# C# D E/B

While many possibilities exist, some may be excluded at first glance as all tones exist in close proximity, which will give the line a fragmented feel, or because all tones exist fairly close to the beginning. Special considerations attend the use of a grouping where the second and succeeding tones exist below the first. Scoring such a collection would mean that either the first tone would act as climax or that an even higher register would have to be opened to feature the second or succeeding tone as the climax.

EX.5

In example 5, above, the climax set consists of pc's 9,7,6, shown scored in two different manners. The second version places pc4 in close registral proximity with pc7, apparently expanding the climax set to become pc's 9,7,4,6. Pc4 may, indeed, be included as an important approach to the tone of climax which latter now functions to close two non-linking versions of the governing set; 9,7,6 and 7,4,6. However, by scoring pc4 to receive little stress, it may be made to function as an intermediary tone, proceeding from pc7 to pc6, effectively excluding it from the set of climax. If pc4 is scored as an internal member of a sub-phrase containing pc's 7,5,4,6 then pc11 must be used to end the line.

EX.6

registral use

The version shown in example 6 presents a more complex use of registers, three in all. The tones in the lowest register carry little weight, primarily serving to approach middle or upper register tones. The middle register contains pc's 9,8,10, a form of 3-2. The upper register contains pc's 6 and 7, with F# receiving the weight of the line, while the pitch climax, pc7, performs a role similar to that of an appoggiatura. The middle pc's 9,11 both receive the weight of their respective fragments, while pc8 serves to prepare the high G.

Eight pc's lie in the lowest register, all of which are involved in forms of set 3-1(0,1,2), as 11,0,10,5,4,3, and 3,1,2. In fact, our line seems to feature a surface of this set. In effect, the line has been broken into three fragments of 4-5-4 pc's. Their respective sets are 0,1,2,3,0,1,2,3,4 and 0,1,2,4I, forming a workable progression.

The upper register tones receiving the most weight are pc's 9,6,11. We have already explained pc11 as completing set 3-2 on the middle level. The Ab and G, which act to prepare F#, combine with A and F# to complete two linking forms of 3-2.

Notice the use of jumps. First is ic+9, followed by ic-11; connecting sub-groups of the line is ic+10, followed by ic+11, ic-14, ic+14; connecting ic-15 and last ic+9. The scheme of jumps exhibits increasing size, with the final ic9 balancing the opening ic9, having been prepared by ic5, the compound appearance of ic3 which is the inversion of ic9.

There is a varied relation of registers, all being contiguous at some point: L-M-L,M,U,L,U,L,M.

rhythm

In many 20th Century styles, there are few examples of a line in regular long-held values. Rhythm is an important factor in conveying the logic of the design. Rhythms should be chosen and combined with articulations to strongly point out tones that are meant to be heard as forming important relationships. In the preceding example, longer values are assigned to significant tones in the middle and upper register and articulation has been employed to refine the perceived succession of 4n-5n-4n sets.

The actual values need not be those shown, of course. However, the consideration of employing rhythm and articulation to project something of our procedures and perhaps even our structural concerns is of great importance.

Whatever the rhythm employed, it tends to wish to re-assert itself continually throughout the work. Here, we are not concerned with the re-use of a specific rhythmic fragment, a procedure to be discussed below, but rather retaining a sense of similarity or flow to successive rhythmic units.

Assn. 6: Re-score the line for several other contours, rhythms and phrasings . Discuss the effect of the various appearances of the line.

Write new lines with set 3-2 or any other 3n or 4n set. Follow the analytical and scoring procedures outlined above.

the revised phrase

As we encountered some difficulties with our previously generated line due to the appearance of non-linked forms of the set in the last half, let us construct a new line, making sure to provide a stronger link between four discrete occurrences of set 3-2.

Beginning on pc's 11,2,1 we again choose to expose one step and one skip for more variety. Let us follow with pc's 10,9,0. While not linking to provide a form of 3-2, these tones do present a retrograde inversion of the first set occurrence.

Combining the two 3n collections yields set 6-1 (9,10,11,0,1,2). We may confine our succeeding pitch choice to the complement, also 6-1, containing pc's 3,4,5,6,7,8. There are few manners in which this set may be partitioned to expose set 3-2, with Ab,G followed by F,E,F#,D# being as plausible a choice as any.

Placing the tones in some order that reflects or expands upon some feature of the opening six pc's is advisable, as such a procedure can affect the large scale procedures of the composition. If placed in order Ab,G,F,E,F#,D# we can reflect several aspects of the opening. First, the descending fragment comprised of pc's 2,1,10,9 of the opening is echoed in varied form by the descending pc's 8,7,5,4.

The first descending fragment presents interlocking ic's 4 – pc's 2,10 and 1,9. This ic is featured to connect the first and last half of the line. The order of the last 3n set exposes a new ic2, and employs ic3 in descent to counter the two successive upward usages at the start of the line. Such considerations at the outset may suggest procedures for the continuation of the work.

EX.7

Analysis of the newly composed line reveals the following sets:

3n   B,D,C#=0,1,3I   D,C#,Bb=0,1,4I   C#,Bb,A=0,1,4   Bb,A,C=0,1,3
     A,C,Ab=0,1,4   C,Ab,G=0,1,5   Ab,G,F=0,1,3I   G,F,E=0,1,3
     F,E,F#=0,1,2   E,F#,D#=0,1,3

4n   B,D,C#,Bb=0,1,3,4   D,C#,Bb,A=0,1,4,5   C#,Bb,A,C=0,1,3,4

     Bb,A,C,Ab=0,1,2,4   A,C,A b,G=0,1, 2,5   C,Ab,G,F=0,2,3,7

     Ab,G,F,E=0,1,3,4   G,F,E,F#=0,1,2,3   F,E,F#,D#=0,1,2,3

5n   B,D,C,E,Bb,A=0,1,2,4,5   D,C#,Bb,A,C=0,1,2,4,5I

     C#,Bb,A,C,Ab=0,1,2,4,5   Bb,A,C,Ab,G=0,1,2,3,5

     A,C,Ab ,G,F=0,2,3,4,7   C,Ab,G,F,E=0,1,3,4,8

     Ab,G,F,E,F#=0,1,2,3,4   G,F,E,F#,D#=0,1,2,3,4

6n   B,D,C#,Bb, A, C=0,1,2,3,4,5   D,C#,Bb,A,C,Ab=0, 1,2,4,5,6

     C#,Bb,A,C,Ab,G=0,1,2,3,5,6   Bb,A,C,Ab,G,F=0,2,3,4,5,7

     A,C,Ab,G,F,E=0,1,3,4,5,8   C,Ab,G,F,E,F#=0,1,2,3,4,8

     Ab,G,F,E,F#,D#=0,1,2,3,4,5

The 3n sets show a consistent use of 3-2 and 3-3, while the 4n sets exhibit a fairly consistent progression around set 0,1,3,4. All but sets 0,1,2,4 and 0,1,2,5, the sets occurring in the middle of the line and linking the first and second halves, are formed of two interlocking ic's 1; 0,1+3,4, 0,1+4,5 and 0,1+2,3. Our 5n sets also reveal strong relationships. We have structured the line to consist of two versions of set 6-1.

While we have assured ourselves that our line exhibits consistency and that surface articulation can employ logical progression and surface variety, again the basic sweep of the line leaves much to be desired. Besides the obvious lack of climax and any real contour, the opening is dominated by successive ic's 3 and the end by a scale-like fragment constructed of alternating ic's 1,2. A redesigned version might appear as follows:

EX.8

First, notice the intervallic connections. In the lower register are ic1 (D,C#), ic3 (A,C) and ic2 (E,F#), the three ic's contained in set 3-2. D,C# link to A# to provide a local-level occurrence of 3-3, as does A,C,Ab between registers. In the lower register 3-3 also occurs as C#,A,C and C#,C,E.

Set 3-2 permeates the entire upper register; B,A#,Ab, A#,Ab,G and Ab,G,F. The opening non-contiguous upper ic1 (separated by ic1) is echoed by a contiguous ic1 approaching the climax. From this point ic2 is featured; in inversion (ic10) to the climax, linked (non-contiguously) F to Eb, separated by ic2.

Assn. 7: Restructure the contour of the line to expose different sets and dominating ic's. Provide good registral use and tones of climax. Employ several different rhythms and articulations to various restructurings of the line.

chapter 4

THE PHRASE GROUP

To this point, we have crafted a germinal line, guided by our stated pre-compositional intent, on the level of note-to-note and set-to-set. We have applied our chosen governing factor within the entire line and among pitches associated by registral placement and articulation. Subsequent lines will continue to be guided by principles of atonal writing and the application of governing factors, but now with an eye to relationships on the level of the entire phrase and among succeeding phrases.

Rather than create a meaningless succession of freely crafted lines, we will develop procedures for extracting materials from the germinal line to inform the subsequent phrase on the level of pitch and set, as well as progression and process. These extracted materials will be expanded, embellished and varied in ways which will enhance the real and perceived relationships within the phrase group or larger sections of the work.

fragment transformation

Our line as it stands represents one phrase of several which will be contained in a phrase-group. Our analysis of the line, both in its scored and unscored versions, have revealed a number of relationships and events, any of which may be featured as the local-level governing factors of a succeeding phrase. In this and following chapters we will explore manipulations performed on fragments or segments of the line and develop procedures to expand, embellish and otherwise vary the fragment while retaining strong relationships to the existing line.

First, we must examine the line for the fragments to be employed. They should be of sufficiently defined character as to retain their identity while undergoing transformation. Cursory study suggests a usage of the three successive 4n sets which were effectively partitioned through rhythm and articulation. These are sets 4-3 (0,1,3,4, pc's B,D,C#,A#), 4-4 (0,1,2,5, pc's A,C,Ab,G) and 4-1 (0,1,2,3, pc's F,E,F#,D#). These fragments may be used to develop strong relationships to the governing set, or to function as the governing set on the local-level. In the latter case, the fragments will be employed to provide strong relationships on the level of set usage, in reflecting the opening line.

These sets each exhibited its own identifiable shape which consists of the order of the elements of the set, and the rhythmic and registral placement of the elements. Let us craft three successive phrases, each based entirely on one of the sets, each retaining the general intervallic-registral contour of the original line. Let the first phrase be generated by 4-3, the second by 4-4 and the last by 4-1, reflecting the order of their appearance in the opening statement.

The opening phrase may be retained at pitch. Such ordered recurrence of an invariant pitch-collection is often featured at structurally significant moments in larger works. The retained pitches may also be re-ordered and still retain relationship to the original shape of ic's 9,1,9, as shown in the four re-orderings below.

B   A#   A#   B   B,A#   A#,B
   D,C#   C#,D   D   C# C#   D

The opening of the succeeding fragment on 4-4 begins with a presentation of the subset 3-3. As this is also a subset of 4-3 we may logically wish to employ an ordering of this subset in reordering 4-3 into the shape exhibited by 4-3. If we reorder the pc's as B,D,A# or as C#,A#,D the set will be completed in a manner more strongly reminiscent of the shape of 4-3 than that of 4-4. Rather than a literal shape, we may reorder 4-3 to provide a similar shape; D,A#,C#,B.

Here, the opening presents ic+8 followed by ic+3, instead of the original ic's 3,8. Instead of ending with ic1, our new order ends with ic2.

The final segment contains, successively, ic's 1,2,3. Set 4-3 contains two versions each of ic's 1 and 3, but only one ic2. This may appear as either C#,B or B,C#. If either is preceded by ic1 or ic3, they will be succeeded by the same interval, and result in a very different shape than that exhibited by 4-1.

ic1,2 D,C#,B,A# or A#,B,C#,D ic2,3 A#,C#,B,D or D,B,C#,A#

The latter are too similar to the opening fragment to be employed here. The others, while not quite duplicating the intervallic surface of 4-1 may be of more value. They may be employed to maximize a surface occurrence of dissonant leaps in substituting for the most dissonant set of the line.

Assn. 8: Reorder the pc's of 4-4 and 4-1 to reflect the intervallic-registral contour of the opening line. Set 4-4 may be represented by its normal and/or inversional form.

Of course, our final form of these phrases would not present three repetitions of the same four pitches. Instead, the collections would occur in the order shown but at some T-level. The vector informs us that set 4-3 retains no new pitches at T5 or T6. If T5 is employed, further transposition by T5 will yield one recurrent pitch, as T5±T5=T10(2). This may be the lesser of two evils as T5+T6=T11(1) which yields two invariant pitches and T6+T6=T12(0) which produces the same four pc's as the opening version of the set. Similarly, set 4-4 can only be transposed once by T6 to provide fresh tones. All other T-levels will result in repeated pitches. Only set 4-1 may be transposed twice and yield all new pitches.

Assn. 9: Provide new transpositions of the successive 4n fragments of each line presenting strong linkage between fragments and to combine climaxes in some strongly presented set.

Combine the original line at pitch with transpositions of the three new phrases to provide strong linkage between the phrases and to present the climax of each line as member of some local or background governing set.

expanded intervallic usage

One disadvantage to employing a governing set of three or four members is a restricted intervallic palette. Larger works would especially suffer from this defect. Rather than create new material to remedy this fault, we could reorder our surface level sets to allow for expanded intervallic usage

Set 4-3 contains an occurrence of ic4 which could be exposed in various ways, either contiguously or registrally associated.

a) A#,D,B,C#	b) A#,D,C#,B	c) B,C#,A#,D	d) B,C#,D,A#
e) C#,B,D,A#	f) C#,B,A#,D	g) B,A#,D,C#	h) B,D,A#,C#
i) C#,D,A#,B	j) C#,D,A#,B	k) C#,A#,D,B	l) A#,D,B,C#
m) A#,D,B,C#	n) D,A#,B,C#	o) A#,D,C#,b	p) D,A#,C#,B
q) A#,D,B,C	r) A#,D, C#,B	s) D,A#,B,C#	t) D,A#,C#,B

Examples a-j unfold ic4 as successive pc's. The reordering could contain ic4 in the same register as the other set members or be placed in its own higher or lower register. Examples h-t are predicated on registral differentiation of ic4, but, again, this new material could be placed above or below the remaining set members.

Each example contains material which bears a greater or lesser degree of similarity to the germinal line. The use of any reordered form to expose new surface intervals should be a conscious and deliberate choice based on the intentions to exploit that particular similarity. For instance, several of the examples begin with three successive pc's which combine to form set 3-3. This is a subset of 4-3 and is featured as the first three tones of the ordering of that set in the original line. If such a reordering were chosen, it would suggest the conscious choice to exploit this common subset and would continue to be asserted in some degree in at least that passage.

Set 4-3 contains not only ic5, but the subset 3-1, neither of which exist in our governing set. These could be featured in reorderings of the set, again choosing that reordering which contains some relationship chosen for exposure. One possibility might contain both the new interval and the divergent subset. If the pitches are placed in order 1,2,0,5 we would emphasize the similarity with the opening three tones of the succeeding set 4-1 which occurs in order as 2,1,3,0. Each contains a similar initial intervallic progression of ic's 1 and 2.

Keep in mind that the new ic's exposed by this procedure will appear at first as anomalies. Unless integrated into succeeding phrases in some way, they will only serve to interrupt the logic and comprehension of the work. They could reappear in any manner or on any level of the work but will definitely wish to assert themselves from that point on.

Assn. 11 Generate the re-orderings of 4-4 to expose ic5. Discuss relationships with the original line and the effect of registral placement. Suggest procedures which might be employed were a particular relationship to be featured.

Only ic6 is not contained as a member of any of the 3n or 4n sets employed to this point. The full intervallic palette necessary for a large-scale work would demand the ability to generate this interval in a manner consistent with previously exposed materials. It may occur as an accident of transposition – that is, it may occur between tones embedded in two successive sets of the same or dissimilar construction by virtue of their pitch contents. The example which follows presents several such occurrences employing transpositions of 4-3.

> at T2 (B,D,C#)A#-E(C,Db,Eb)
> at T1 (D,C#)B,A#-E,F(C#,D)
> at T5 (B,D)A#,C#-E,G(D#,F#)

Re-ordering the intervals could place ic6 as the link between succeeding T-levels. The new ic could be associated by placement in high, middle or low register.

New intervals could also be generated by expanding the sets. In the case of 4-3, for instance, pc's 3,4 could recur as 0,1 of a new occurrence of the set. In effect, this is a transposition by T3 which our vector informs us will result in two repeated pc's. These two intersecting transpositions have provided both ic's not found in the original set. Other possible intersections are shown below.

0,1,3,4	0,1,3,4	0,1,3,4	0,1,3,4
0,1,3,4,6,7	9,10,0,1,3,4	0,1,3,5	0,1,3,4,5,7,8
0,1,3,4	0,1,3,4	1,2,4,5	0,1,3,4
		0,1, 3,4	

Set 4-3 is symmetrical; that is, it exhibits the same successive intervallic content if read from right-to-left or left-to-right. Set 4-4 is not symmetrical. This means that not only does it generate an inversion distinct from the prime form, but that intersection may occur between prime and inversional forms, as well as the manner of intersection applied above to set 4-3.

> 9,[0,1,2,5] 8,11,[0,1],2,5 9,0,[1,2],3,6 0,1,2,[5],8,9,10 0,1,[2,5],6,7

Assn. 12: Construct various intersected sets on set 4-4 in the manner employed for 4-3. (i.e., consider 0 as 1,2,5 of the prime or inversional form, 1 as 0,2,5, etc.)

Construct symmetrical and expanded intersections of sets 3-3 and 3-2, employing prime and inversional forms.

Discuss the relationship of the intersecting sets with the original and with aspects of the germinal line. Examine intersections for the appearance of subsets of previously employed sets and for new 3n and 4n sets.

chapter 5

THE EMBELLISHED LINE

<u>basic procedures</u>

Our original line may be expanded through embellishment. This consists of adding new tones which will associate with intervals of the germinal line to maximize the appearance of some important local – or large-scale set. Let us employ 3-2 in this capacity.

Both opening ic's 3 could complete a form of 3-2 with pc0. Featured at the mid-point of the opening fragment, C would embellish the movement from pc's 2,1 while acting as the link between two intersecting occurrences of 3-2 (11,2,0 and 0,1,10).

EX.9

Both examples above present registrally associated forms of 3-1, a subset of 4-1, while retaining the exact ordering and registral placement of the original line. The second version also contains a shape in the upper register which reflects the opening three pc's of 4-1; ic1 and ic2. The second four pc's form the new set 4-2I (0,1,2,4). The entire fragment combines to form 5-1.

EX.10

Pc0 could also be employed as a boundary to the phrase. The second scoring in example 10 employs the boundary pitch repeated in the highest register. The effect of that re-use and registral placement is markedly different from its appearance in the in the lowest register, as the higher register carries more weight. Indeed, when pc0 bounds the phrase in the highest register, that pitch is emphasized as seemingly the most important tone of the phrase, relegating the original fragment to a secondary level of prolongation. In either case, a recurrent progression of ic's 1 and 2 is featured.

We may choose to embellish the registrally distinct tones into their own statements of 3-2. Pc's 11 and 10 could complete 3-2 with either pc's 8 or 1, Ab or C#: pc's 2 and 1 are completed by pc's 4 or 11. The last example below combines the first two and adds pc7 as the final tone, completing 3-2 with pc's 8 and 10. The middle members, pc's 1 and 2, were arranged to avoid perception of the E major or G# diminished triad. While a G minor triad now occurs as the last three tones, there is enough previous conflict to obscure its appearance. Occurring in the second inversion also decreases its strength. While such traditional constructions are avoided on principle, they may occur if they are the natural outcome of the local procedures, always providing they do not destroy the texture of the phrase by asserting their identity too strongly.

EX.11

Such procedures could be employed to maximize any set, either agreeing with the fragment it embellishes or being some other previously employed or newly generated set. For instance, set 4-3 may function to maximize its appearance and embellish each succeeding fragment.

EX.12

Assn. 13: Analyze the above fragments. Determine the associative procedures employed to generate maximal occurrences of 4-3. Discuss the relationships of the new line to the original and the effect of registral placement and rhythm.

Employ the first, third and fourth fragments above in a single continuous line keeping the ordering shown intact. Transpose the fragments to provide relationships among the most strongly stressed tones of each fragment and, if possible, to counteract any closely recurring, easily perceived invariant tones. Restructure the rhythm and provide articulation to heighten the design or to separate accidental fragments which conflict with the prevailing intervallic texture.

The first fragment above associated B and D with C and Eb, and C# and A# with A and C to present a maximally embellished presentation of 4-3. The resultant pitches might suggest a re-ordering which would link a newly generated pitch to a pitch of the original to provide a similar but not transpositionally exact contour. The new pc3, for instance, could be placed in conjunction with pc2 of the original collections, repeating the placement of the descending ic1 of the original but in varied relation to its surroundings.

EX.13

Assn. 14: Analyze and discuss the above example. Provide similar re-orderings of all three embellished fragments of the original line. Link the three fragments, providing strong relationships among stressed tones of succeeding fragments through transposition.

<u>the nested pitch field</u>

The example below illustrates a more complex pitch-field generation which charts maximal occurrences of 4-3 in relation to every contiguous ic of the original line. This process is sometimes referred to as nesting. First level generations, that is those that form 4-3 with the pc's of the original line, are shown immediately below the original pc's. Second level generations proceed from the combination of one pc from the original line and one from the first level. In some cases, a third level generation, maximizing the first level into a new version of 4-3 is shown. Of course, this process could be continued indefinitely and provide any number of generational levels to maximize any set or group of sets.

B	D|D	A#|A#	A
C,Eb	Bb,B/E,F	C,A	F#,G
Ab,A,F,F#		Eb,E F#,G	
C# E			

A   C|C   Ab|Ab   G
   G#   B   A   B   E,F Bb,B
F,F#   D#,E   C#,A#   G,Bb
   G,Bb

Great care must be exercised in attempting to score such a complexity of tones. The greater the number of pc's generated, the greater the possibility that the controlled and orderly flow of the work may be lost, buried beneath ever more dense clusters of sound. Of course, that might suit your compositional intentions, but the purposeful obscuring of controlling factors is seldom in the best interests of the cogent presentation and communication of musical thought.

In setting such an array, score the generative tones – the ic's of the original line – in a manner that stresses their importance and retains their association. This could be accomplished rhythmically, dynamically, registrally (not necessarily in the highest register), by virtue of occurring as the first and last tones in the sub-phrase, or by articulation. Remember, the generated tones are meant to embellish the pre-existing line and should be heard as progression from and to the generating pc's.

Next, present the nested tones in some manner which intentionally reflects and exploits some factor or relationship.

EX.14

The 3n groupings in example 14 consist primarily of 3-2 and 3-3. Each set occurs twice in 4-3, as a normal and inversional form. The accidental sets of 0,4,8 and 0,2,5 also occur. The pitches are ordered to first present the shape of the second segment of the original line extended by a second contiguous jump of ic8. The following tones, pc's 1 and 3, complete an initial collection of ic-2, ic+3, ic+8, ic+8, ic-3, ic+2. The fragment beginning on pc3 is a transposition of the original form of 4-3, ordered to culminate on D.

The next group will be employed as an approach to C#, beginning on B in the same register as its previous appearance in order to reassert, briefly, its importance. Each pitch of the opening ic5 forms ic1 with one member of the following ic5 and ic6 with the other. This serves to effectively counteract the apparent Bb minor triad of the last three tones. C# appears as ic1 below C, linked in the same register as they were in the original.

EX.15

The descent from C# to A# completes the nested presentation of 4-3, placing the tones in their original order, with ic's 11 and 10 registrally linked but the whole having undergone a registral transposition. The successive 3n sets of this group balances those of the first, in reflection of pc's 1 and 10 balancing the generating pc's, 11 and 2. They are 3-2 (including pc 10 of the previous group),10,1,0; 3-2, 1,0,3; 3-3, 0,3,4; 3-3, 3,4,7; 3-2, 4,7,6; 3-2, 7,6,9; and 3-3, 6,9,10.

There is a reflection of the previous group employed to approach C# – 0,1,5,6 – fashioned to occur in various hidden but strongly associated manners throughout the phrase. The first occurrence is comprised of the two separated occurrences of ic1 (pc's 1,0 and 7,6.) The second version is interspersed between these ic's and consists of the two downward ic's 11 (pc's 3,4 and 9,10) as do the middle four – 3,4,7,6. Each presentation is formed by two versions of ic1 linked at T3. The boundary set employs these pitches in presenting ic's 1 and 11, the middle set presents them as ic's 11 and 1.

These boundary and nested forms of 4-3 exist at T6, hence the occurrence of intervallic symmetry and the existence of set 0,1,5,6. This simple transpositional usage is mitigated, somewhat, by rhythmic factors. The unfoldings of 4-3 also show a resemblance to the shape of the original appearance of this set, although reordered. Pc1 proceeds to pc4 – a downward ic9 – by way of pc's 0 and 3, here as the inversion of ic9.

Ic1 will dominate the setting of the next group, as well. Rather than combining to form any regular set usage, it will be employed to form various subsets reflective of aspects of previously exposed collections. Pc's 9,8,6,5 present 4-3 as a simple downward progression. The succession of ic's is 1,2,1,2, with the last two ic's presenting the subset 3-1. The following sixteenth note flourish exposes its ic's 5 and 7 (with connecting ic4) in a manner reminiscent of the occurrence of set 0,1,5,6 in previous groupings. The quicker rhythm here is intentionally employed to emphasize the first and third tones of the collection, heard as an embellished ic1 from pc10 and 11.

This perception of Bb connecting to B occurs simply because the ear has been focused to hear the eighth note throughout the previous unfoldings. Therefor, the motion from the opening A to the final C is heard as being connected by a simple ascending chromatic motion.

EX.16

The succeeding group dovetails on C and presents three occurrences of ic9 to reflect the germinal setting of 4-3. The registrally distinct pc's each form 3-1, exposed as successive ic's 1 and 2, reflecting the importance of the chromatic set in the previous group. Notice that the second level generation of G was not employed. This was intentionally excluded in order to expose the features described above and so that G may connect with the last Ab of the sub-phrase in the same manner and function as in the original line.

EX.17

The last generation presents pc's 10,11,4,5, the exact pc's used to approach C# near the beginning of this scoring of the nested pitch-field generation. There they appeared in the order of pc's 11,4,5,10,1. Here they are re-ordered pc's 5,10,11,4,7, a transposition of the original occurrence at T6. The invariant 4n collection forming 0,1,5,6 was fashioned to present a recurrent shape and function, rather than to present them in the same order and register, as was the case with the more closely positioned invariant pc's 7,6,9.

The entire line appears as follows:

EX.18

Registral use, by sections, is L-M-H; L-M-H; H-M-L; M-H, H; M-H. The lowest register appears primarily in the first third of the piece, the middle register is featured in the middle third, and the last section exists primarily in the upper register, with the overall sweep of the line reflecting very strongly the varied registral use of the first fragment. The lowest register unfolds a chromatic set, as do the climaxes of the first fragment. We have already noted the occurrence and importance of the chromatic sets and ic1 in the middle and end of the line.

The middle register is dominated by the chromatic set comprised of pc's 4,5,6,7,8,9 – set 6-1. The first fragment presents the subset 3-2, the second 4-1 ordered to produce the normal and inversional forms of 3-2. Pc9 is asserted at the end of this fragment as a member of 5-1 and inversionally related forms of 3-2. This dovetails into 4-1. The recurrent pc9 serves to link the middle and upper registers which have retained discrete identity to this point. Notice the insistence of pc's 10 and 11 from here to the end of the phrase.

Assn. 15: Complete the maximal generation of 4-3 nested in the original line. Score the pitches consistent with procedures and concerns discussed in setting the above. Employ set 4-4 to function similarly in generating a nested pitch-field.

chapter 6

TRANSFORMATIONS AND VARIANTS

inversional, registral, and intervallic exchange

The following procedures go beyond the expansion or embellishment of partitioned segments and will produce transformations or variants of the original sets. The first procedure employs the same ic's of the original but not the same direction, and will be termed interval exchange. Under this operation, the opening order of 4-3 becomes +/-9,+/- 1,+/-9. This generates the following pitch collections, all proceeding from pc11.

    B(+9)G#(+ 1)A(+9)F#   B(+9)G#(+ 1)A(-9)C   B(+9)G#(- 1)G(+9)E
    B(-9)D(+1)D#(+9)C   B(±9)G#(- 1)G(-9)Bb   B(-9)D(+1)D#(-9)F#
    B(-9)D(- 1)C#(+9)A#   B(-9)D(- 1)C#(-9)E

Assn. 16: Apply this procedure to the ordering of segments based on 4-4 and 4-1.

A further variation would substitute the inversion of the pc's shown, resulting in no new pitches but new contours for each permutation. Each will present different possibilities due to registral placement. This will be termed registral exchange.

EX.19

The sum total of this process might be described as the free directional and inversional exchange of members, and be represented as, say, + or – 3 or 9.

The final variational procedure consists of a more extended re-disposition of intervals and will be called intervallic exchange. There are several possibilities. The first is to exchange ic1 for ic2, ic3 for ic4, ic5 and ic7 for

ic6 (or ic5 for ic6 and ic6 for ic7). This would transform the various segments as follows;

4-3	B,D,C#,A# = B,D#,C#,A (4-21; 0,2,4,6)
4-4	A,C,Ab,G = A,C#,A#,G# (4-3; 0,1,2,5)
4-1	F,E,F#,D# = F,Eb,E,C (4-6; 0,1,2,7)

This manipulation will produce a different resultant pitch collection for
each possible ordering of the set contents. Unwonted duplication of some
pc(s) may occur.

4-3	A#,B,C#,D = A#,C,C#,D# (4—10; 0,2,3,5)
	A#,B,D,C# = A#,C,E,D (4-21; 0,2,4,6)
	A#,D,B,C# = A#,C#,A,A# (3-3; 0, 1 ,4)
	A#,D,C#,B = A#,C#,B,A# (3-2; 0,1,3)

Assn. 17: Complete the permutations of 4-3, subjecting each to intervallic exchange and calculate the resultant sets. Do the same for 4-4 and 4-1.

Consonant/Dissonant Exchange

Another useful intervallic exchange is to substitute "dissonant" intervals
for "consonant" ones: ic1/ic3, ic2/ic4, ic6/ic5. The two examples below show
the effect of such exchange on the partitioned segments of the germinal
line and on the same permutations of set 4-3.

4-3	B,D,C#,A# = B,C,A,G#	4-3
4-4	A,C,Ab,G – A Bb,Ab,F	4-4
4-1	F,E,F#,D# = F,D,F#,F	3-3

4-3	A#,B,C#,D= A#,C#,F,G#	4-26 (0,3,5,8)
	A#,B,D,C#= A#,C#,D,B	4-3
	A#,D,B,C#= A#,C,A,F	4-14 (0,2,3,7)

Assn. 18: Following the directions for assn.17, complete the process for
4-3 and apply to 4-4 and 4-1.

Either or both types of intervallic exchange may be coupled with inversional and/or registral exchange, producing a myriad of variations and transformations of the appearance of chosen fragments. The resultant collections could be employed "as is" to produce great variety and/or be coupled with earlier procedures. Pitches may be generated to expand, embellish, or to produce nested materials, and may serve to heighten differences or to bring these new and greatly varied materials back under the sway of local or background controlling factors.

refinements of contour

In the last several chapters we have developed procedures for the expansion, embellishment and variational transformation of a given fragment or shape. The perceptive student may be aware that each procedure often yielded similar sets or collections. This should not be surprising as the use of each technique was guided by similar concerns, applied to similar sets.

The combination of the specific intervals of a line and the generation of pitches to fulfill surface or background presentation of specific sets will generate similar pitches by the very nature of interval and pitch content of those specific sets. However, the importance and function of the pitches generated will differ. Therefor, while the pitch collections exhibited some similarities, their appearance and contour, as well as the general effect of the resultant lines, each displayed a distinct character. This was conveyed through the use of rhythm and register. Each rhythmic and registral setting was chosen to more clearly present our intentions and the processes employed.

Compositions consist of more than just pitches and sets. The sense of a composition is conveyed on more levels than the surface of note-to-note. Contour, that is, the rhythmic and registral shape, refine the presentation of the pitches generated, exposing relationships hidden in the line and placing stress on tones chosen for their importance in exposing relationships and procedures. In effect, contour allows us to clearly communicate the function not only of pitch but of process. Rhythm and register, as well as further refinements of articulation, are more than accidents of scoring or mere local level occurrences. Their use is a vital part of the overall communication of our compositional intent.

traditional variants

It might have been noted that the concepts of inversion, retrograde, and retrograde-inversion were not discussed as an important technique. These procedures are strongly featured in a great many works and will be presented in succeeding chapters. Here, they were consciously avoided.

There is a great pitfall attendant on the use of these rather simple formulations. While they can be consistently applied with comparative ease, they do not necessarily guarantee clear communication just by virtue of their use. This is especially true when applying these manipulations to larger collections.

Our pitch generations and/or scorings have included some fragments which could be described in terms of these procedures. They may be considered a special case of the procedures developed previously: that is, not only were the pitches generated by a procedure that yielded a great diversity of pitch collections, but that the procedure also resulted in an order which might be the retrograde, inversion, etc, of a given fragment. In such cases their appearance was dependent on and refined by other larger scale controlling factors of background and/or local level set usage, procedures and contour. When they occur as the outcome of some procedure – that is, by intention and design – and are guided by such larger concerns, they may prove to be a very valuable addition to our arsenal. Without such controlling factors they may lull one into thinking that relationships have been developed and successfully employed.

chapter 7

INTERSECTION

We will now develop procedures based on cornmonalities between the sets of the line, and extend the procedure to affect the recurrence of re-ordered pitch contents in succeeding phrases. Comparing the three 4n sets of the original line, we might notice that sets 4-3 and 4-4 contain the common sub-set 3-3, and that 4-4 and 4-1 both contain 3-1. Let us employ these sub-sets to intersect the 4n sets. Using pc's 1,2,4 to project 3-3 at the point of intersection, 4-3 would be completed by pc3 and 4-4 by pc11. (The inversion of 3-3, 0,3,4, could have been employed as well, with pc's 0,3,4 completed by pc's 1,5.)

Placing the common sub-set in the central position gives the pc's the order of Eb,C,C#,E,B. Let us fashion the collection in some manner which recalls the opening phrase but which is not identical. The original unfold-ing of 4-3 produced ic's 9 (down) and 9 (up), bounded by first and last notes at ic1. Many permutations of the intersected set progression may produce similar shapes. The following was chosen for its similar contour but dis-similar intervallic construction.

EX.20

Comparing this to the opening fragment of the original line, we notice that each contains a jump down from the first pitch and a jump up to the last. First and last jumps were originally ic9; here they are ic11. Both surround a downward moving ic1. The first three tones of the original form set 3-2, the last form 3-3. Here the first through third tones form 3-2, the second through fourth form 3-3 and the third through fifth form 3-1. In addition, the three middle register tones form 3-2.

This seems to fulfill our needs in terms of contour, interval and set content. However, the actual pitches must be transposed so that pc3 does not occur so close the last tone of the original, where D# was featured in the role of climax. T2,3,4 each result in a recurrence of pc3, as does T11. T2,4,5,6 all result in a recurrence of pc5. At T10 no recently used pc's recur; C#,D,B,A#,A.

The last three tones can serve as the intersecting point between 4-4 and 4-1, the latter of which can be completed by either Ab or C. The Ab is less desirable for a number of reasons. First, it would result in a fairly simplistic unfolding of descending ic's 1, although differentiated registrally. Also, the previous tones contain two ic's 11, placing a great emphasis on the disparity of register. Using C would balance the upward ic9, D to B, with the downward A to C. Where Ab would link 3-1 to 3-1, C produces 3-2. The beginning pc1 and the highest tone, pc9, both of which receive aural importance due to placement, combine with C to form 3-3. Last, employing Ab would result in a 6n set of Ab,A,Bb,B,C#,D (0,1,2,3,5,6), while C gives A,Bb,B,C,C#,D (0,1,2,3,4,5), the exact set formed by the first and last six tones of the original line. Our line now exhibits set 4-3 intersecting with 4-4 by way of 3-3, and 4-4 intersecting with 4-1 by way of 3-1. The 4n sets occur in the same order as in the germinal line.

We may confine our search for the following pc's to the complement of those pc's already used. They are D#,E,F,F#,G,G#. Such transpositionally (or inversionally) related complements are commonly employed in serial and atonal composition.

Of these tones, only G# provides a line with A and C which can be justified in terms of previously occurring sets. In fact, our original phrase also contained A,C,Ab as the fifth through seventh tones. Here, they appear in opposite direction.

Let us employ a different ordering of sets in the second half of this phrase, this time intersecting only two sets:

$$D\#,E,F\#,G\# = 4\text{-}4$$
$$D\#,E,F\#,G = 4\text{-}3$$

This possible organization of the tones gives one version of 4-4 and one of 4-3. As we know that we must begin this fragment on Ab in order to form a strong link with the preceding fragment, and that Ab is involved with 4-4, our progression of sets will form an "arch"; 4-3, 4-4, 4-1, 4-4, 4-3.

If D# and E are central, then Ab must be followed by F. To succeed F with E will necessitate registral shift on D#, a repeated climax if the jump is upward. By choosing D#,E we retain some freedom. Now we have only to decide on the order and register of the remaining two tones, F# and G. Used in that order, the last five tones would be F,Eb,E,F#,G, an intervallic progression of ic's 2,1,2,1. If reversed, the last three tones would change to

E,G,F#, ic's 3,1, which would balance the previous ic3(9), Ab,F. Placing F#
above G gives A and F# as climaxes to the line, an interval of 3-2 not previously occurring in the register of climax of our germinal line.

re-ordered partitions

A comparison of our two phrases will show some points of interest. The
new line of the phrase-group is, in effect, a re-ordered partitioning of the
4n, 3n, and 5n collections of the original.

EX.21

Let us apply similar procedures to the third and final phrase of our opening
phrase-group. This time, we will employ the same partitioning of the total
chromatic while re-ordering the contents of the 4n groups of the original
line. We must provide a different appearance to each group and climax
tones, attempting to find tones which will convey some local or large scale
concerns.

EX.22

The first four tones re-order 4-3 to expose new ic's 2 and 4 around a central
ic1. Coincidentally, pc's 11 and 1 were the first pc's of the first and second
phrase, respectively. The contents of 4-4 are separated by a quarter note
rest, with pc's 0 and 9 following pc10 to form 3-2, which also appeared
as the first 3n sub-set. The upward jump from pc0 to 9 refers back to the
original opening. In neither the previous newly generated line nor in this
one does the original shape of ic+9, ic-9 occur. Rather, the previous line
employs ic-9, and this line is generated by ic+9. Both lines employ pc's 0,9
in this context.

The lowest register of the first half contains only ic3, with 3-2 occurring in the middle register. Pc9 combines with the middle register set to produce 4-3. The entire collection forms 6-1. The intervallic succession of the opening is echoed and expanded in the opening of the second half. First ic's 14(2) and 11 were presented; the second half presents ic's 11 and 10(2). Each opening fragment employed a repeat, first of a single pitch, then of the interval ic11. Their effect is to suggest a slowing of the line by reiteration and insistence, as well as the rhythmic values employed.

The first two pc's, 7,8, link across the rest to complete 4-4. The first and last 3n set of the second half exposes 3-1. A middle register presentation of 3-2 is formed of pc's 7,6,4. Combining these pc's with the final middle register pc5 yields 4-1, as do the last four contiguous pc's. The two pc's preceding the climax combine with the climax in 3-2, as occurred in the first half of the line. Each ic2 approach to the climaxes completes 0,2,4 with the previous tone; pc's 2,10,0 and 8,6,4.

The lower register of the second half contains only pc8. This forms ic3 with the lowest pc of the first half, just as that pc generated ic3 in the lower register with pc2. The apparent ic6 between the low register pc2 of the first half and pc8 of the second is an echo of ic6 between the pc's of climax. The climax of the second half combines with the middle register of the first to present 3-2, comprised of pc's 1,0,3.

Pc9, occurring as the climax of this line, also occurred as an internal climax in the preceding phrase. There, it occurred in the middle register and was employed to approach the true climax of the line on F#. Here, it does not represent a re-used tone of climax, as its function and placement differ greatly from its previous appearance.

The combined climaxes of our phrase-group are pc's 5,3; 6; 9,3. The first two groups present a form of 3-2. The combination of the pc's of any of the governing sets cannot include ic6. However, the pc's forming ic6, A and D#, stand in the same relationship to the F# climax of the preceding phrase as the D and Ab of the lower register of the last phrase do to the opening pitch B, in that they surround the beginning pitch with ic3 to either side.

The only aspect of this line which may be seen as presenting any serious difficulty is the repeated occurrence of pc3 as climax toward the end of the first and last phrases of the group. This fault is mitigated by the distance between the re-use as well as its surroundings. Also, in the first phrase, pc3 was presented in the highest register of the line; here it is associated in the middle level.

Even if such a recurrence is felt to be a serious defect, the line may still be retained if transposed to expose new pc's for the climax. The simplest manner in which this may be accomplished is to transpose the tones of climax of this phrase to provide some justifiable set membership with previous climaxes. Then apply the T-level under consideration to the opening of the line, choosing that T-level that not only combines climaxes strongly, but presents relatively fresh tones for the opening. Be aware, however, that a transposition of the line will destroy the "echo" of ic+&-3=6 existing between climaxes of the last two phrases and the lower register of the last phrase. It will also greatly modify our design of re-ordering the pitch content of the original set presentation.

chapter 8

EPISODIC VARIATIONS

A composition consists of the formulation and communication of musical ideas. These ideas inform every level of the composition. As previously stated, some conception of the piece must exist prior to the actual writing even if it merely consists of the choice of a governing set and the instrument you wish to write for. All the factors to be discussed below go into the work as a whole, but may not have been pre-conceived. As more experience is gained, it is possible to progress from the reactive – that is, generating pitches first and deciding on their use after, to the tactical – generating pitches to perform a specific, preconceived, local level function – to the strategic – hearing the piece as a whole in greater or lesser detail before composing, and generating pitches to fulfill the functions of the fully conceived structural design.

Our composition will take the form of episodic variations. Episodes are units of form in which a fragment extracted from the line generates the variation. The fragment should be of sufficient character as to retain its recognizable characteristic's while undergoing expansion, embellishment or transformation. It may be chosen for and feature set content, contour, intervallic content, or rhythm. These characteristic's may be projected singly or in combination.

Each succeeding episode is generally of a different character, but this difference may be subtle or blatant. However the succeeding sections may relate or contrast, a general plan of events will help provide continuity of logic and progression of events. We will return to these vital considerations affecting structure and form, below.

instrumental considerations

To begin with, we will limit our choice of instrument to a single woodwind. "Doubles" should be employed only if the piece is of sufficient length to absorb the diversity of color, and the piece is so structured that a pronounced span of silence does not disrupt the flow of the piece while instruments are being changed.

Be familiar with the character, abilities and limitations of the instrument. Be sure the piece is playable. It is surprising how many "professionals" produce scores which ask for notes outside the range of the instrument. Worse still, performers are asked to produce "ppp" in ranges where "f" is comfortable and "mf" difficult. Perhaps the most common failing is to compose a line which lies well under the hands and sounds well on the piano, but which is awkward, uncomfortable, difficult or impossible on the chosen instrument. Also, reliance on synthesizers is fostering an approach to instrumentation based on "realizing" scores by programming the unreal, non-idiomatic lines possible on the keyboard. In actual performance, such minutely "realized" compositions give surprisingly different effects, due to problems of balance, dynamic's, ensemble and timbre not occurring in the studio.

Find a performer to try out passages which appear difficult. Ask for suggestions when real difficulties are encountered. Often a difficult passage is easiest transposed by even one half-step. Performers are often eager to share "tricks", easy techniques that produce difficult sounding results, or even to explore new possibilities for the instrument.

Failing to find a performer, at the very least refer to manuals of instrumentation and orchestration, listen to works which feature the chosen instrument, with score if possible. Purchase a handbook of fingerings and check the diagrams to see what changes the hands must make. Remember, your piece will be performed by a human being, not a machine. It must capture his imagination before he will choose to spend long hours in rehearsal. Besides being musical, your piece must be notated so that the performer may grasp your intentions. Only then will he feel capable of adequately understanding and conveying your intentions. Few performers will go so far out on a limb with a difficult piece as to damage their reputation.

the compositional plan

There are many ways to begin organizing a composition. The following plan breaks the process down into manageable units. Not all steps need be followed, nor must they be completed in order. Read the section carefully, making sure all the steps and their purpose is clear. If you wish, you may develop your own plan of attack, but be sure you account for all of the steps outlined below.

Once the germinal line has been composed and analyzed, enough information should have been gathered to suggest a number of fragments which might be extracted and/or sets to be featured. Discern the factors that suggested each fragment and exploit them to influence the character of each episode. You may wish to feature more than one fragment in one episode and to plan for a final episode in which all fragments will appear.

Define the character and contents of the episode as clearly as possible. You may have a hazy conception of some facets of the episode, but having at least some general idea from which to work will be of great benefit. The following is a broad outline of the parameters to be considered. Your preliminary concept may be general or specific.

1. Activity: fast/slow; silence included?; regular or irregular rhythm, meter

2. General character: agitated, placid; loud, soft; constant or changing texture

3. Set usage: background or local level; procedures; new sets

4. Pitch generation: based on germinal, how?; by what procedures

5. Contour: special gestures or type of motion; registral use and function

6. Instrumentation: special technique, colors

form and structure

Now that possible procedures and characters of the episodes have been considered, we must return to the germinal line. At present, it probably consists of only one phrase which may be expanded into a phrase-group. The succeeding phrases of the group should be strongly related to the opening line but should begin to reflect the characteristic's to be featured in the episodes. Also, if the germinal line exhibited specifically designed progression on any level – rhythms progressing from slow to fast, texture from simple to complex, registers from high to low, etc. – reflect this as well on that same level in the succeeding phrase of the opening phrase group.

Just as our note-to-note choices were guided by a logical flow, so must all aspects of a composition be in service to a feeling of progression from one point to the next or later points. The concept of progression guides the motion between successive notes, climaxes, sets, fragments, phrases, phrase-groups, and sections throughout the entire work.

EX.23

Episode	_____
Group	_____ _____
Phrase	_____ _____ _____ _____ _____
Climax	_____ _____ _____ _____
Set	__ __ __ __ __ __ __ __ __ __
Pitch	_ _ _ _ _ _ _ _ _ _ _ _

Once the opening phrase group has been completed, plan a tentative order in which the episodes will appear. Not only will you want to provide this scheme with a progression from episode to episode, but you will want to allow for moments of dramatic tension. The scheme of episodes should also be a reflection of local level and large scale usage.

You may wish to plan a return to a simple or simply varied restatement of the opening material at structurally or dramatically important points of the composition. This allows the ear the re-focus on pertinent materials before beginning a new procedure or development. These interspersions may function as ritornelli or as intermezzi.

Just as our background level set informed our composition on the level of note-to-note, so will our controlling set and the concomitant structure of the phrase inform every level of the composition. We have already discussed the composition of the first phrase group and the reflection of characteristic's of the first phrase to succeeding phrases. The ordering of the episodes should be planned so that the progression to succeeding episodes reflects something of the progression from phrase-to-phrase or fragment-to-fragment.

For instance, if the first phrase group exhibits growing activity, a plan for succeeding episodes might reflect that growing activity in the character of the episodes. There might be a plan for alternating episodes of more-then-less activity. The episodes may be ordered to present an arch form, beginning with less activity, progressing to very active sections, and finally to less active sections. But do not plan too simply. Even in an arch form, it is possible to "nest" an episode of a divergent character within the form. Remember that just as anomalous tones are impressed more strongly on the ear, so do anomalous events imprint the piece.

However, a poorly placed or structurally obscure event will imprint just as strongly, but negatively, in the overall comprehension of the piece.

One episode should be planned which recombines the extracted fragments and refers to the various procedures employed. At first glance, it might be assumed that such an episode must feature a great deal of activity and many pitches. While that may be your choice, consider that a simple texture of few notes can accomplish the same task. All that is necessary is that procedures and activity be absorbed.

If you choose to present the last episode as very active, you may wish to plan a coda of short length to absorb the active texture of the terminal episode. The character of the coda must be chosen to fulfill a perception that structural closure has been achieved.

Each phrase group and episode should contain one climactic pitch and be associated with the climaxes of its own and accompanying phrases as previously discussed. The climax of each structural unit – phrase-group, episode, section – should be associated with one another, just as they are within the phrase.

The piece should also contain climaxes of drama, procedures, rhythmic activity (or repose), dynamic's, insistence through repetition (invariant usage), perhaps even silence; in short, of any characteristic of fragment, procedure or surface event. In general, they may be conceived as being a maximal statement of some facet of the composition or procedures other than pitch.

There should be a climax to the entire composition as well. While this generally occurs at the end of the piece, it often will be placed near the end, instead. This could be the coda, the terminal episode, or some preceding episode. A position near the end is favored for the same reason that pitch climaxes do not occur too early in the line: once the climax has been reached it is difficult if not impossible to retain the listeners interest.

rhythmic variation

Some special considerations are necessary when a fragment has been chosen for development by virtue of its rhythm. It is possible to apply the concepts of augmentation, diminution and retrograde to a given rhythm. These are rather simplistic procedures and can be very effective, but a simple insistence on such procedures in a full episode would, perhaps, result in too regular and predictable a texture.

Like the rhythmically-based variations of earlier ages, it is possible to present a constant texture of some rhythm to contain the varied and expanded pitch material. This may affect a fragment or the entire line.

If you choose to feature such a section, be sure to avoid regular rhythmic recurrence. Also, be sure to space points of stress at non-regular, non-repeating rhythmic positions in the line.

Perhaps of more interest than either regular, constant rhythm or the applications of retrograde, augmentation or diminution is to apply procedures developed for handling pitches. It is possible to feature an exchange of rhythmic units, as shown below, or by any other exchange factor.

EX.24

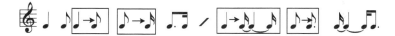

The rhythmic units can be retained, but re-ordered.

EX.25

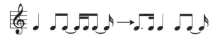

Nesting, either of a full group or a fragment of a rhythmic group within a rhythmic group of larger values, can not only provide rhythmic interest but can function to contain a second level pitch generation or any subsidiary, linking or recurrent materials.

The rhythmic group may be freely varied by several procedures. The expected occurrence of a rhythm may be anticipated;

EX.26

A value may be extended – suspended – past its expected end;

EX.27

One or more shorter values may embellish the beginning or end of a longer value;

EX.28

Stress can be retained on the original rhythmic placement of the line while a subsidiary rhythm may be interpolated and used as a passing rhythm.

EX.29

event analysis

Analysis on the level of event is not only of great value in structuring the unfolding of a piece, but is one of the most important listening tools that can be developed. If practiced faithfully and diligently, event analysis will become an automatic process and will continually add to your compositional awareness. It is an indispensable tool in gaining insight into modern works, especially as scores are seldom available for more detailed study.

When hearing a piece, discern first the character of the sections. The character is a reflection of the surface activity – rhythmic, textural and timbral. These facets may be involved in presenting very varied settings, either homophonic, contrapuntal, or the setting of a distinct melody and differing accompaniment. The types of setting may be involved in exposing, developing, or simply re-using previously exposed and/or developed material in a new and varied format. Theremay be conscious and deliberate re-use of specific materials, heard as discrete events by virtue of rhythm, pitch choice, instrumental usage or existence in a particular register. New material may be evolved by processes of embellishment, expansion or variation with a new or recurrent surface activity on some level.

Each piece contains material specific to that piece which governs the unfolding of the piece on one or more levels, either rigorously applied or affecting only the surface. This material may be defined by any of the facets described above.

With such event analyses, we are less concerned with hearing minutiae than with gaining an overall sense of the dramatic or constructive form of the piece. Hearing on the level of note-to-note and chord-to-chord is an added important consideration, but not strictly necessary. Such abilities gained through ear training studies will enable you to hear more specific detail and will inform you of specific procedures on the level of pitch. However, event analysis is concerned more with the relation of succeeding structural events.

As you become more versed in listening to the structural unfolding of events, you will become more impressed with the similarity of compositional concerns throughout the entire span of musical history. Procedures relating to surface content and pitch choice may change for every era, while structural procedures remain the same, perhaps expanded, varied or even re-defined.

For instance, while the form of a symphony may be subjected to a textbook analysis and be concerned on some level with the importance of key scheme, such tonal procedures do not directly apply to 20th Century concerns. However, the presentation and unfolding of sections will present a flow of events towards some goal. These events may succeed each other subtly, or by a surface character which differs in some lesser or greater degree. The dramatic effect of succeeding sections tells us about the specific intentions of that particular composer and piece at hand, but is also a general statement of compositional and dramatic structuring of materials, regardless of the express concerns of that era, style, school or composer.

Even a key-oriented composition may hold important information on the level of pitch which may be applied to contemporary methods of pitch generation. One must merely be aware of the structural or dramatic usage on the level of pitch and be able to extend pitch procedures by analogy into the current pitch vocabulary. A moment in, say, a Beethoven piano sonata which employs pitch choice – i.e., key area or motivic transformation, or any other pitch-oriented concern – in order to further a dramatic or structural design may be applied to atonal materials by applying a similar procedure to contemporary pitch choice.

Each succeeding age redefines pitch choice and usage – modal, tonal, atonal; homophonic, contrapuntal, developmental. Instrumental choice and usage also change. While textbook descriptions of the forms employed throughout the history of music stress changing considerations, the application of form is always in service to the presentation and comprehension of materials as a flow of events toward a goal. A well-structured form presents a work in an orderly progression of events to be comprehended as a complete and satisfying whole. This general definition applies equally to Bach and Beethoven, classic or modern, solo or orchestral. Analysis at this level continually refines one's compositional sense and expands one's structural and formal vocabulary. Every piece you hear can refine your sense of the compositional process. Everything is grist for the compositional mill.

Part 2
Multi-Voice Composition

Chapter 9

TWO-VOICE WRITING

General Principles

We will now develop procedures for setting the original line against an added voice. Primarily, we will be concerned with retaining the primacy of the original line, allowing it to sing through a multi-voice texture. With few additions or modifications, the added voice will be guided by the same principles as were applied to single line construction.

The use of contrary and oblique motion is favored where strong linear independence is desired. Similar motion may be employed freely and will result in a less obviously independent coupling. Parallel motion is reserved for use only when some over-riding dramatic or structurally significant moment demands it. The mixture of various types of motion is a decision based on the degree of independence desired in the added voice.

Voice crossings tend to blur the outlines of the separate voices and should be employed, again, only when some significant moment may benefit from its use. Instrumental color, articulation, dynamic's, etc, can do much to focus the ear to the actual linear progression at the point of voice cross, mitigating the blurred contours.

Voice exchange – that is, the immediate repeat of a pitch from one line in the other – may be employed freely in the added voice. When the added voice presents the specific pitch first, the primacy of the original line is somewhat weakened. Such usage should be approached with care. In either case, the result is a blurring of the distinct contours of the lines and, in effect, produces a perceived slowing of the pace of pitch succession.

The added voice may contain any number of pitches, fewer or more than the original line. Also, pitches may recur with considerably more freedom in the added voice, especially when the original line contains all twelve tones. In such a case, the original line will provide the re-used pitch with a new intervallic coupling, thus altering its surroundings, effect, and function.

Models of Two-Voice Procedures: 1 vs. 4

Our first settings will employ as few pc's as possible in the second voice. This allows the original line to retain its importance and structural strength, while the longer-held pc's of the second line are given more time to impress the ear. Let us attempt to combine each 4n fragment with one held tone. Let 3-2 be projected as the controlling factor in the pitch choice of the second line, as well.

As was discerned earlier, the opening four pc's which present two successive ic's 3 may be maximized in two versions of 3-2 by pc0. Let this begin the second line. Now some pc must be chosen to follow pc0 which projects some interval of 3-2 as well as combining in justifiable relation to the following four pc's 9,0,8,7. Of the possible choices, pc's 1,2,3 will be discarded as they form new sets with the original. Pc9 occurs in the original voice and may be employed only if the unison is desired. It will result in sets 3-3 and 3-3, both justified as significant sub-sets of the 4n sets of the original line.

EX.30

Pc10 will combine with pc's 9,0,8,7 to form two successive occurrences of 3-2. As this pc has just occurred in the original line, it can only recur here as a voice exchange in the same register as its previous appearance. Otherwise, a severe registral shift and voice cross will occur which will mask the contour of the original, presenting a perception of the original line shifting from the upper to lower position.

EX.31

EX.32

Use of this pc will result in parallel ic's 1, hidden by virtue of the intervening pc's and the appearance of the first ic as a simple interval while the second is a compound (ic13).

Pc11 may be employed, forming sets 3-2 with pc's 9,0, and 3-3 with 8,7. While pc11 began the original, its re-use occurs after the use of five intervening tones, counting pc0 of the second line. Its first occurrence produced ic1 vertically and ic3 horizontally. Here it forms ic2(10). Notice the hidden parallel ic's 1-0 occurring at the end of the first 4n group (pc's 0,10 forming acompound interval and 11,9 occurring as a simple interval.)

EX.33

If the second line consists of pc's 0,9, the last 4n fragment must be coupled with either pc's 10 or 11 in order to form 3-2 in the second line. Neither pc results in justifiable set or intervallic combinations with the last group. If pc0 is followed by pc10, only pc's 9 or 1 will complete 3-2. Again, neither results in a useful coupling.

Pc's 9 or 2 will complete 3-2 with pc's 0,11. Pc2 results in 3-2 with pc's 5,4, and 3-3 with pc's 6,3. The second voice presents ic's 1 and 3 contiguously, with an overall motion of an ascending ic2.

EX.34

While both climaxes occur at the same point, both approached from below by skip, the seeming dependence of the second line's climax is mitigated by several factors. First, pc2 is approached by a small consonant leap while pc5 is gained by way of a wide dissonant interval. Second, pc5 does not receive the same weight, as it tends to a resolution on pc3.

The vertical intervals formed at the point of attack of the second line exhibit a progression of intervals from dissonant to consonant. The first is ic11 (compound), an inversion of ic1. The second, consisting of pc's 11,9, forms ic10, the inversion of ic2. The last presents the double compound of ic3. This progression of ic's 1,2,3 exposes the entire intervallic content of 3-2.

Assn. 19: Combine the original line (or any other previously composed line) with various 3n sets. Let the added voice project 3-1, 3-2, 3-3, and combine with the original to produce justifiable sets or to project some new set or sets which recur throughout the setting.

Now let the second line contain four pc's. Again, let us begin with pc0, forming 3-2 with 11,2,3-1 with 2,1, and a combined set of 4-1. The following pc's 10,9,0 can combine with pc's 1 or 11. If pc1 is used, the combined set of 4-3 occurs as the combination of two forms of 3-3. However, this necessitates not only a voice exchange and a voice cross, but the shift of the opening pc0 up an octave to avoid the awkward jump of ic13.

EX.35

There are several points to be considered. First, the voice exchange occurring so close to the beginning of the line casts the added voice in a more subservient role than if the line were given several pc's during which to establish its independence.

Second, the voice exchange produces a slowing of the rhythmic texture at the outset. If coupled with the original rhythmic setting, the influence of pc1 is extended to last for a combined length of six consecutive eighth-notes. The lack of motion at the point of voice exchange gives the ear a moment to orient before the voice cross occurs. Were this to be employed, the independence of the lines would necessarily require some refinement of articulation, timbre, attack or rhythm to clearly define the lines and mitigate the blurred contours at this point.

Pc11 could also be placed in this position, combining with pc's 10 and 9 to form 3-1, with pc's 9,0 forming 3-2, and would project a combined 4-1. This is the exact set usage of the first setting, occurring in reverse order on the level of 3n sets. There is a parallel ic11 occurring at the beginning of each 3n setting. This, and the re-use of pc11 are hidden by intervening pc's and the upward jump of ic9 against the downward moving ic1 of the second voice. The previous ic1 of the original voice approaches the coupled pc's 11,10 to form set 3-2.

EX.36

Pc's 8,7,5 can combine with pc's 4 or 6 to form the best possible set usage. As these pc's will be featured strongly in the last 3n fragment, their use here would weaken the primacy of the original line. Also, pc6 does not form any interval of strongly occurring sets with any pc of the second line.

Either pc 2 or 9 can complete useful sets with pc's 0,1 or 0,11 of the added voice, but pc2 forms no strongly occurring sets with this 3n fragment. Pc9 forms 3-1 (7,8,9) and 3-6 (5,7,9). These same sets occur if pc2 is set against the last 3n fragment of pc's 4,6,3. Set 3-6 previously occurred as a registrally defined set, consisting of pc1 approaching the second pitch placement of pc11 and followed by pc9. This elevates the registral, accidental occurrence of this set to a surface level occurrence.

EX.37

If pc's 9 and 2 are used to complete a line begun by pc's 0 and 1, sets 3-3 and 3-4 (9,1,2) occur contiguously, with 3-1 occurring over the entire sweep of the line (0,1 ,2). If used to follow pc's 0,11 sets 3-2 and 3-7 occur contiguously with an overall motion of 3-2 (0,11,2).

EX.38

The first setting shown in example 38 presents ic's 1,3,1,2 at the points of attack, exhibiting a graceful progression of intervallic tension. The intervening ic's expose different vertical combinations for each successive 3n fragment, with a recurrence of ic's 4 and 1 following the attack of the second and fourth pc's of the second voice, producing an intervallic echo which functions to strengthen the relation of first and second halves of the line.

The second setting shows a division of vertical intervallic structures in the first and second halves of the line. The hidden parallelism at the beginning of each of the first three fragments is a liability if strongly independent lines are desired. However, this may also be viewed as a simple imitation of the long range motion of the line, functioning to underscore the real motion from fragment to fragment. If this imitation were to be pursued, it might be useful to provide pc8 of the original line with somewhat more weight than in our original setting, so that a perceived long-range motion of ic5 from pc's 8 to 3 is heard as strongly functional, placing more actual importance on the motion of ic5 in the accompanying line from pc9 to 2. If the original scoring of the lines is retained, the "imitation" of ic5 remains in incipient form, to be featured or suppressed in following sections.

Assn. 20: Add a second voice consisting of four pc's. As in assn. 19, use 3-1, 3-2, 3-3 or new sets which recur throughout the setting.

shaping the second voice

The use of ic5 to accompany the second half of the line suggests another possible approach. As longer, more involved compositions may benefit from the introduction of new ic's, their exposure and development in the second voice or occurring between the lines is a natural and logical procedure. As the first and second halves of the original both present 6-1, mere transposition will yield pc's to form ic5 while presenting symmetry of set and interval content in first and second half settings. First and second forms of 6-1 occur at T6. Applying this T-level to pc's 9 and 2 results in pc's 3 and 8. Pc3 can accompany the first 3n fragment to result in 3-3, 3-1 and 4-2; pc8 combines with pc's 10,9,0 to form 3-1, 3-3, 4-2. The shape of the second line now presents a contour reminiscent of the opening 4n fragment, a rather more loose application of imitation with considerably more perceived independence between the lines. Two interlocked forms of 3-5 occur (pc's 3,8,9,8,9,2), combining in 4-9 (2,3,8,9).

EX.39

Assn. 21: Apply the above considerations to introduce new intervals and/ or sets in the second line, displaying symmetrical and non-symmetrical structures.

<u>1 vs. 2</u>

Now let our second line present one pc to accompany two successive pc's of the original. The controlling set(s) of the second line must include ic's 1,2,3, as these are the intervals occurring between pc's of the original. The 3n sets 3-1, 3-2, (3-3, partially,) will fulfill this requirement.

If we begin on pc0 to form 3-2 with pc's 11,2, we are faced with extending pc0 to accompany pc's 1,10 or re-using pc11, now after only one intervening tone. Pc's 1,10 cannot be combined with one pitch in the accompanying line to form set 3-3, as both pc's which will complete this set have already been used – one just before, and the other just after these two pc's. Let us defer pc0, then, to occur against pc's 1,10, forming 3-2.

The first two pc's cannot, then, combine with any pitch to present 3-2, as both possible pc's will occur immediately following. They can be combined in set 3-3, instead. Pc10 will follow directly, leaving only pc3 to occur with pc's 11 and 2. This will result in a progression of ic3 in the added voice from one occurrence of 3-3 to one of 3-2.

EX.40

The remaining dyads of the original can all be completed in 3-3, placing pc1 against 9,0; 11 vs. 8,7; 8 vs. 5,4; 7 vs. 6,3. The line which results projects 3-2 in the first half of the line and 3-3 in the second. Its full analysis is shown in example 41.

EX.41

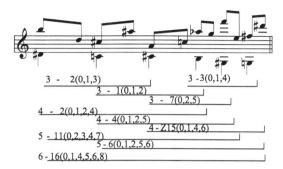

A very strong, real independence is exhibited by this combination. First consider the intervals which occur at the point of attack. The first half presents ic's 4,1,4. The two occurrences of ic4 are actually at T2 but this is hidden by the octave difference in their spacings. The second half presents parallel ic's 3 but so scored to hide this parallel relationship, as well. Considering the second pc of the original with the pc's of the added line, there exists a hidden parallel ic1 (11) at the point of the second and sixth pc's of the original. These are far enough apart and their unstressed occurrence mitigates the parallelism. Similarly, the parallel ic's 3 and 4 existing against pc's 11 and 8 of the added voice is surrounded by so much disparate activity that the parallelism is effectively countered.

The first and second pc's of the added line form a consecutive ic1 – actually ic's 11 and 13. The motion of the upper voice is a descending ic1 against the added voice, forming a descending ic3. The independent intervallic movement, even though in similar direction, nullifies any feeling of parallelism. No other subsequently occurring intervallic repeat occurs in the two voice structure.

Strong sets are also evidenced by the combination of the even numbered pitch placements of the original line with the following simultaneous attacks, as shown in example 42.

EX.42

Assn. 22: Provide a similar coupling of two original tones against one in the added voice. Project only set 3-2, then 3-3. Complete one more coupling which uses sets 3-1, 3-2 and 3-3 freely.

held or repeated tones

The second line may freely hold pc's and provide fresh ones for combination with individual pc's of the original. This allow for considerably more freedom in pitch choice as a given pc of the added line need only combine justifiably with one pc of the original and present a contiguous intervallic motion which may be justified on the local level of pitch-to-pitch, or some larger level as included in some unfolding of governing sets.

Consider the following:

EX.43

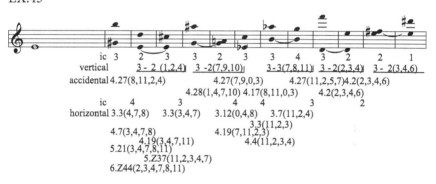

ic	3		2		3		3		2		3		3		4		3		2		2		1	
vertical			3 - 2 (1,2,4)		3 -2(7,9,10)			3-3(7,8,11)		3 - 2(2,3,4)		3 - 2(3,4,6)	
accidental	4.27(8,11,2,4)					4.27(7,9,0,3)			4.27(11,2,5,7)	4.2(2,3,4,6)	
					4.28(1,4,7,10)	4.17(8,11,0,3)			4.2(2,3,4,6)	
										4.2(2,3,4,6)	
ic	4			3			4			3			2	
horizontal	3.3(4,7,8)		3.3(3,4,7)		3.12(0,4,8)		3.7(11,2,4)	
							3.3(11,2,3)	
	4.7(3,4,7,8)			4.19(7,11,2,3)			
		4.19(3,4,7,11)			4.4(11,2,3,4)	
	5.21(3,4,7,8,11)				
		5.Z37(11,2,3,4,7)			
	6.Z44(2,3,4,7,8,11)				

Besides the analysis given above, notice the emergence of set membership in the combined registers. Opening pc8 connects registrally with pc's 7,9=3-1. Pc9+pc's 0,11=3-2. Pc's 2,1+0,11=4-1. Registrally, the second line projects 3-3 (8,7,11) and 3-1 (4,3,2). The last pc4 is "unconnected"to the second line, but connected by voice exchange with the original.

Assn. 23: Create several lines of various numbers of pc's to combine with one or more original tones. Feature relationships of set usage in some lines, exposure of new materials shaped to reflect the contour of the original in others.

  Subject the added lines to justifiable registral permutations. Discuss the results.

Begin the second line one and two octaves higher. In effect, a T-level of 12 places the second line in the same register as the original; by T24, the added voice becomes an upper line. Discuss the results.

note-against-note

Our second line will now be crafted to present each pc of the original with its own accompanying pitch. We will choose pc's not only for their vertical results with the original and horizontal in their own line, but also for the 3n sets formed with surrounding pc's.

Let pc3 begin the line, forming 3-3 with pc's11 and 2. The opening pc's can form 3-3 with pc0 as well. Let pc0, then, combine vertically with pc2. Our second line now contains pc's 3 and 0. This can form 3-3 with pc11 (already used) or pc4. Combining pc's 1 and 4 gives ic3 vertically, 3-3 with pc0 of the previous interval, and 3-2 with pc2.

EX.44

There is no way in which pc4 may combine in a 3n set which includes the following pc10 of the original to form any previously employed sets. Also, as all pc's which can fulfill our set requirements with pc's 1 and 10 of the original line have either already occurred or will follow pc10 closely, this pitch will be combined to present an interval which can combine with following pc's in a strong set statement. Pc's 10 and 9 of the original can form 3-3 with pc 3 or 6. As pc3 began the line, let pc6 accompany pc10.

EX.45

Notice the reliance on similar motion. This is mitigated by the varied vertical intervals employed - ic's 4,2,3,4 - and the dissimilar linear intervallic motion; ic-9 vs. ic-3, ic-1 vs. ic-8, ic+9 vs. ic+2.

Just as the opening ic4 was followed by the specific pitches which completed two linked forms of 3-3, occurring as ic2 (pc's 0,2), let pc's 6,10 be followed by pc's 9,7.

EX.46

The following pc0 can combine with pc8, forming 3-3 (9,0,8) and 3-1 (7,9,8). This places pc8 immediately prior to its occurrence in the original line. This very close re-use need not be discarded as neither tone receives any stress and, therefor, do not greatly impress the ear. In fact, its recurrence emphasizes its transitory function. Setting pc8 in the original against pc11 saturates this complex of tones with strong set usage, completing 3-3 (7,8,11), (0,8,9),; 3-1 (7,9,8); 3-2 (9,8,11), (9,0,1), (6,8,9).

EX.47

Pc11 can be held to combine with pc7 forming 3-3 with two consecutive pc's of the original. Similarly the following pc's 5,4 can be combined with pc1 and the last pc's 6,3 with pc2. Pc's 1 against 5,4, and 2 against 6,3 each combine in 3-3. The added voice pc's 11,1,2 form 3-2. This is a very dependent line, placing all emphasis of motion, contour and pitch generation on the original line. A less dependent line is possible.

EX.48

Pc7 of the original may be coupled with pc3. Set 3-3 occurs in the added voice. The climax of the original, pc5, is coupled with pc2. The following pc4 combines with pc's 2,5 to present 3-2.

EX.49

If pc4 is combined with pc1, the latter forms 3-3 with the previous vertical pc's 2,5, and with the melodic pc's 4,5, as well as 3-2 with pc's 2,4. The
following registral contour will serve to disguise the chromatic descent of
the added voice.

EX.50

Setting pc10 against pc6 completes 3-3 (2,1,10). If the final pc3 is combined
with pc11, an apparent "V-I" progression will result. Pc0 will counter this
tonal usage. Our lines now appear as follows:

EX.51

Notating the two lines on one staff reveals a common register containing the lower register of the original line and the upper register of the added.

EX.52

The added voice exhibits several re-used pc's and contains no upper climax. As it stands, the lack of climax forces the line to occur below the original, whose climax functions for both lines, with the second line merely providing accompaniment at that point.

As the added voice is dependent, its pc's receive their registral stress and weight by virtue of their association with truly stressed pc's of the original line. Therefor, the opening pc3 and 6 which follow receive stress. The later occurring pc's 3,2 - positioned before and at the point of climax-receive registral stress, as well as pc2 gaining importance by accompanying the climax. These four pc's combine with the earlier pc's to form 3-3. Pc's 3,2 unfold a line which ends with pc0 accompanying pc3 of the original with this last tone receiving associated stress, and forming 3-2.

Assn. 24: Compose a note-against-note two voice coupling which exhibits maximal usage of sets 3-1, 3-2, and 3-3.

<u>second line climax</u>

If the added voice is to occur above the original it must be constructed to contain pitch climax. The following example couples the lines at ic's 3 and 4 only. The upper line presents very few previously occurring sets. Instead, they are formed by combinations of pc's of both lines.

EX.53

Assn. 25: Construct an added voice above, providing good climax. Decide on sets to be employed and the manner in which they will be formed.

chapter 10

REFINEMENTS OF THE TWO-VOICE MODEL

cartwheel motion

The use of held tones allows more than one pitch to occur against any other tone. This suggests the further possibility of allowing the added voice to present several pc's against a longer held pc in the original line, resulting in a "cartwheel" motion. Example 54, below, illustrates this procedure.

The added voice answers the jumps of the upper line with a similar jump. The following rhythmic figure is scored to suggest similarity with the opening fragment of the upper voice, forming a linear occurrence of 3-1 while combining with the held pc10 to form first 3-2 and then 3-3. The whole forms 4-2. The voice cross at the point of connection between the first and second 4n fragments of the upper line is made easier to follow due to the held tones preceding the voice cross.

The lower line now presents a linear unfolding of 3-2. The held pc4 completes 3-3 with the following pc's 8,7 of the original. Pc7 serves to connect to the following vertical placement by way of 3-6 which recurs in the next fragment (pc's 4,6,8). Sets 3-1 (5,4,3) and 3-2 (3,4,6) occur as the combined sets of the line leading to the final activity of the lower line which, in turn, projects 3-3 (8,0,11) and 3-4 (0,11,8). 3-4 begins and ends the line and is arranged to expose the relationship. The inter-linear set is 3-3 (0,11,3) with the final pc7 completing a registral 3-2 with pc's 4,6 of the upper voice, and a contiguous occurrence of 3-3 (6,3,7) distributed between the lines.

Adhering to the rhythmic scoring of the original line causes the embellishing pc's of the second line to be compressed into units of rather short duration. In applying this procedure, the rhythm of the original might be revised to provide more longer held values against which the added line might interpolate more graceful rhythmic units.

EX.54

Assn: 26: Employ the above procedure on the original line, freely revising rhythm to accommodate the interpolation of rhythmic units of the embellished added voice. Be sure that rhythmic activity is rather evenly distributed between the lines and the phrasing and connections of the rhythmic units focus the pitches to serve the logic and design of the lines. Employ any set(s) in recurrence throughout.

anticipation and suspension

Just as rhythm was employed to refine our single line, so it may be used to function in a similar manner for multi-voice writing. Besides rhythmic procedures previously discussed in this and earlier chapters, pitches need not be attacked simultaneously in both lines. Rather, a pitch may enter earlier – in anticipation – or later – as a suspension – than its accompanying pitch. This is akin to held tone usage and should be employed in like manner, occurring when the relationship of a given pc to more than one accompanying pc is to be featured.

In example 55, holding pc3 from position 1 (the first "measure") to the second heightens the perception of 3-3. The delayed occurrence of pc5 associates with pc's 2,3 to project 3-2. Pc5 occurring against pc's 2,1 yields 3-3. Pc7 in positions 4 and 5 combines with pc's 10,9 to form 3-2, etc.

EX.55

Assn. 27: Employ anticipations and suspensions on examples or completed exercises from the previous chapter to heighten the perception of set. Allow new sets to occur by means of anticipation and/or suspension only if they may be caused to reappear by similar means (as in the case of 3-8 at the end of ex.55.)

interpolation

As lines may be embellished and more than one pc may occur against any longer pc, new pc's may be interpolated between existing ones. This is an especially fruitful procedure when a line exhibits few controlling sets, as in ex.55.

EX.56

Assn. 28: Find the pc's which were interpolated into the upper line in the preceding example, and discuss the new sets formed in the upper voice and between the two voices by their addition. Employ this procedure on any previously or newly composed two voice structure.

imitation

Notice that the upper voice of example 56 relies primarily on ic2 in the opening half and ic1 in the second. This is suggested by the first three pc's 3,5,4 (ic+2, ic-1). The re-use of specific intervallic motion throughout a line is employed as a major factor in imbuing a line with identity, much as the similar reliance on the larger intervallic content of set adds coherence. This constitutes a form of imitation, freely employed, on an identifiable shape presented in a secondary line.

Assn. 29: Refine the previously completed assignment, or any other two-voice structure to present a shape which recurs throughout the embellished line, represented by all or part of its intervallic content.

A secondary line may employ imitation of some aspect of the primary line. This involves both lines in the presentation of the same materials, strengthening the importance of a single idea. This imitation can be more or less exact and still be heard as an insistence on some similar material or procedure.

Imitation can exist on the level of set. The examples below employ a form of 4-3 in the secondary line to accompany the presentation of that same set in the original. In both cases the shape and intervallic unfolding of the set differs from its appearance in the original.

EX.57

This type of imitation guarantees a consistent intervallic texture when not only do the upper and lower voices project the same sets, but when the pitches are unfolded to feature strong subsets vertically. Here, the accompanying pc's are offset rhythmically to strengthen the presentation of such vertically occurring subsets. The first is designed to answer the downward moving half-steps with ascending ones. The second presents a compressed imitation of the shape of the upper line.

As the second example above suggests, general shape or contour may be the basis for imitation, in a rather more identifiable form. Set 4-17(0,3,4,7) is employed in example 58 to imitate the contour of 4-3. Both fragments employ a downward jump followed by ic1 and an ascending jump. The original intervallic fragment is employed to link the first and second 4n fragments of the original, placed against the held pc10.

EX.58

Set 3-2 is formed by pc's 10,8,11. Two forms of 3-3 are presented in the secondary line, linked by pc's 11,0. Exposing the imitation by placing it against the held tone allows the ear to focus on its shape without the distraction of accompanying pitches. As the shape is a similar but not exact imitation, the emphasis allowed by this placement gives time for the relationship of the fragments to be clearly discerned.

A secondary line may present a fragment which imitates the intervals of the primary line. Both fragments above (exs. 58b,c) are ordered to present the same intervallic succession. The first, employing set 4-3, presents ic3, an inversion of ic9 of the original. Set 4-19 in the second fragment presents the same intervallic succession as the original but with very different contour. When the imitation of a fragment occurs simultaneously with the presentation of the fragment it imitates, the imitation still exists but the ear will be less likely to comprehend the relationship which exists between the lines. This hidden imitation can be used to great benefit in providing a strong textural and contextual identity. More often, however, imitation is offset, exposing the process.

Assn. 30: Discuss the above examples. Place the fragments at any T-level against the various pc's of the original in any rhythm. Discuss the results. Construct new fragments to imitate the general contour of complete or partial fragments, or even to imitate a succession of contiguous pc's drawn from successive fragments. Place these against various pc's of the original.

The final and most specific form of imitation is an exact recurrence of shape, intervals and set. An entire line may be imitated exactly, with all pc's of the secondary line existing at the same T-level from the pc's of the original line. Each fragment may exist at a different remove from its original, rhythmically or transpositionally. The same fragment may recur throughout.

EX.59

Exact imitation can be modified by retrograde, inversion or retrograde-inversion.

EX.60

Assn. 31: Construct various added voices, each constructed to emphasize a different design of imitation, as described above.

Example 61 presents the line accompanied in its entirety by various forms of imitation.

EX.61

Pc's 0,8,7,11 present two forms of imitation. They are ordered to invert the shape of the original fragment, while the last three pc's imitate the last three of the original on the level of set (3-3). Here, the intervals are ic's 8,1, varying the ic's 9,1 of the original, answering set 4-3 with 4-7. Pc11 in the second voice connects with pc's 3,2 to form another occurrence of 3-3. With the following pc0, a full imitation of set 4-3 – the opening 4n fragment of the line – is completed. The imitation at this point is rather more complex, existing on several levels. First, holding pc11 against pc's 8,7 of the upper voice and connecting to pc3, presents an inter-linear imitation of the opening 4n fragment in inversion. The intervals are ic9 (compound), ic1, ic4 (ic8 inverted; compound)

EX.62

The shape of the pc's from pc11 to pc0 imitates that of pc's 0,8,7,5 on the level of shape, not set. The first ic4 is formed by pc's 11 ,3 and is an inversion of ic8, which is found in the original as pc's 0,8. pc's 3,2,0 imitate pc's 8,7,5 exactly. A registrally associated shape consisting of the previous pc's 7,3,2,0 combines to form an imitation of the shape of the opening 4n fragment.

EX.63

The ending pc's 2,0,10,1 present a simultaneous inversional imitation of the last fragment of the original. pc's 2,0 imitate the descending ic13, while the last three pc's are an exact inversion.

EX.64

The descending half-step is featured throughout both lines, as shown in example 65, below. Also, the lowest three pc's, 0,11,1, imitate the intervallic succession of the middle register of the original.

EX.65

Assn. 32: Create one or more second lines saturated with various forms of discrete and interlocking imitative figures. Let the lines combine in strong sets, or at least strong intervals. Analyze and discuss the results.

chapter 11

THE NATURE AND USE OF DISSONANCE

Multi-voice settings follow the same principles of movement and connection which govern single and added voice writing. Pitch choice should reflect controlling sets. Motion between pc's of a given line should result in varied contour by virtue of vertical intervallic combinations and direction. Employ contrary and oblique motion where possible, similar when necessary, and parallel only when specifically required by constraints of the line, set or imitation, or when intended for structural or dramatic purposes.

Simple voice-leading may employ oblique motion in connecting two successive forms of the same set or two different sets by relying on invariant pc's.

EX.66

The above examples, while employing primarily the same sets, produce markedly different results. This is due not only to the pc's generated by the moving lines and the contours of the lines themselves, but to the spacings of the trichords, as well. In example 67, below, set 3-2 is presented in its various spacings. Their perception as tense or relaxed is directly related to the intervals which occur between adjacent pc's.

EX. 67

A collection may be projected as primarily consonant or dissonant by virtue of spacing.

EX.68

The Basis of Perception

The great variety of spacings possible, combined with the successive occurrences of dissimilar sets, demands the development of some procedures to guide and control their unfolding and use. In some respects, contour, imitation and the logic of pitch choice will act to inform the appearance of specific spacings. However, some conception of the nature and perception of the incipient dissonant-consonant content of sets and intervals is invaluable, especially when balancing sets of greater pitch membership and density.

Many explanations for the cause and effect of our perceptions of consonance-dissonance have been advanced throughout the course of music history. Most rely on either "ratios" or stylistic usage. Ratios suggest that the placement of an interval in the harmonic overtone series is an indicator of its effect, with more complex ratios resulting in more dissonant intervals. Reliance on stylistically-derived usage orders consonance-dissonance on a contextual basis, with the most dissonant intervals being those that most strongly demand a change of mode or tonal center.

Each approach presents difficulties as both rely on abstractions and are not related to the realities of musical performance. Reliance on ratios measures the occurrence of some interval against a phantom fundamental. For instance, the tritone is explained as the ration 5:7; that is, as occurring as the fifth and seventh partials above a fundamental. In performance, a tritone may be projected without the lower fundamental. The ratio is merely a mathematical description of the relationship of the frequencies at which the two tones vibrate.

Stylistic usage describes the perfect fourth as dissonant in some circumstances and consonant in others. Also, the tritone, especially above a given tone, or in relation to a given tonic, is considered in some systems as the most dissonant interval. In every case, explanations based on stylistically derived tonal usage related specifically to that particular style and era and are not based on the projection of a "sound ideal" of that particular period. That is, they are predicated on principles of chord construction and succession, and relationships within and among keys and/or modes.

intervallic order

With several significant exceptions, the prime intervals exhibit increasing consonance in direct relation to increasing size. The most consonant interval is the octave, the unison being excluded as there is no distance – interval – to measure. Next follow, in order, ic's 7, 5, 4, 3, 9, 8, 6, 10, 11, 2, 1. The consonant intervals appear before the tritone, the dissonant after. With the exception of the p5/p4, the simple intervals are stronger in effect than their inversions.

P8	p5	p4	M3	m3	M6	m6	A4/d5	m7	M7	M2	m2
Ic 12	7	5	4	3	9	8	6	10	11	2	1

The order in which the intervals are presented is based on the actual occurrence of musical performance. In reality, every pitch is the fundamental of its own overtone series. Rather than existing in relation to a specific key or "phantom" fundamental, the effect of an interval is directly related to the degree of agreement of the overtones generated by each pitch.

The higher an overtone series is projected or calculated above its fundamental, the more partials there are within the octave. The occurrence of a given pc in a lower register allows more partials to be projected in the audible range. Therefor, in widely spaced intervals there is more likelihood of the partials generated by the higher pc agreeing with those of the lower in the register where their partials overlap. Closely spaced intervals, especially in the lower registers, are often described as "muddy". This is due to the great amount of partials projected in the audible range. In fact, it is very difficult to discern the identity of very closely spaced intervals in very low registers due to the great amount of agreement of partials in the audible range, as well as the relatively small difference in the vibration frequencies of the pc's.

dissonance factors

A simple procedure to measure the inherent tension to set contents or their spacing may be employed, which will assign a numerical representation to the various intervals. This will be referred to as the "dissonance factor". This is a simplification in that it does not consider differences between simple, inverted, or compound forms.

The unison and octave is assigned a dissonance factor of 0, as there is no disagreement between the overtone series of this interval. Ic5/7 will be assigned a factor of 1, ic4/8=2, ic3/9=3, ic6=4, ic2/10=5, and ic1/11=6.

Let us apply dissonance factors to the first four trichords, all forms of 3-2, in the preceding example. The first two spacings employ adjacent ic's 1,2, with a dissonance factor (df) of 5+6=11. The first is slightly modified by the presence of compound intervals. The third projects ic's 8,13; 3+6=9. The last employs ic's 14,9; 5+3=8.

Assn. 33: Calculate the dissonance factors for all previous example in this chapter. Place in order from high to low.

Score a mixed collection of 3n sets in various spacings. Calculate dissonance factors and place in order of increasing dissonance.

df: inherent and by spacing

Dissonance factors play an important role in ordering the appearance of sets of differing intervallic content and/or with sets of different amounts of members. For instance, the sets 3-1, 3-2, and 3-3 exhibit df's of 17, 14, and 11, respectively. Set 3-1 contains two ic's 1 with a factor of 6 for each. The remaining ic2=df5; 6+6+5=17. Set 3-2=([ic1=]6+[ic2=]5+[ic3=]3=14).

> 4-1(0,1,2,3)=(0,1=6, 1,2=6, 2,3=6,0,2=5, 1,3=5, 0,3=3)df31
> 4-2(0,1,2,4)=(0,1=6, 1,2=6, 0,2=5, 2,4=5, 1,4=3, 0,4=2)df27
> 4-3(0,1,3,4)=(0,1=6, 0,3=3, 0,4=2,1,3=5, 1,4=3, 3,4=6)df25

Notice that the calculation of the inherent dissonance factor of a set includes every interval of the set, while the dissonance factor for specific spacings excluded the interval formed by non-adjacent, "outside", voices. Were that interval to be included in calculations, all spacings of the same set would be equal, which the above examples shows is not the case.

comparison and projected factors

It is possible to compare either the inherent or spacing df of sets of dis-similar size. For instance, sets 3-1 and 4-1 are both formed by successive ic's 1, a simple chromatic fragment. The inherent dissonance factor of 3-1 is 17, comprised of three intervals, icl twice and ic2. 4-1=df3l, comprised of six intervals. By dividing the sum of dissonance factors by the number of intervals calculated to arrive at that sum, the relative dissonance of each collection can be compared. Therefor, 3-1 exhibits a relative df of 17 divided by 3=5 2/3, one of the most inherently dissonant of all sets. 4-1=df3 1 divided by 6=5 1/6. 3-1 approaches the df of icl(df6), while 4-1 is slightly more dissonant than ic2(df 5).

Dissonance factors allow us to compare the actual spacing of sets of dis-similar numbers of members.

EX.69

The first set in the example above, 3-2, is spaced to expose adjacent ic's 3 and 1. With the following sets, all comprised of more than three members, calculating only adjacent intervals will give a somewhat limited picture of the full effect of the sonority. It will, indeed, give an accounting of the ef-fect of the strongly heard adjacent structures, which color our perception of the projection of the set as primarily consonant or dissonant, but does not present the full effect of the chords tension.

To complete the picture, all internal intervals, that is, the less exposed couplings of non-adjacent intervals including at least one inner voice, should also be included in calculations. Therefor, while the adjacent intervals of the second set, 4.2, yield a factor of 10, comprised of the three ic's 2,2,1, the projected dissonance of the set includes ic's 2 (Pc's 8,6) and 1 (10,9), as well. The full projected df of this specific spacing of 4-2 is, then, 21, compared to its spacing factor of 10 and its inherent factor of 27.

Set 3-2 exhibits a spacing factor identical to its projected factor of 9, comprised of two intervals which yield a comparison factor of 44. The spacing factor of 4-2 is 10, comprised of three ic's yielding a comparison factor of only 3 1/3, a rather wide shift of tension from 3-2. The projected factor of 21, a sum of the five internal intervals, gives a comparison factor on the level of full projection of spacing/contents of 4 1/5, rather more similar in character to the comparison factor for this specific appearance of 3-2. Therefor, while the adjacent strongly perceived intervals of 4-2 give a much more consonant presentation to the set, its full projection links it rather gracefully with the preceding 3-2. The comparison factor of the sets are 3-2=4 2/3 and for 4-2=4 1/2.

Assn. 34: Calculate the inherent, spacing and projected dissonance factors of the 5n and 6n sets above. Reduce each to a comparison factor.

Re-order the contents of the four sets to project the most dissonant (highest) factors, and again to project the most consonant (lowest) factors. Arrange the resultants to project a gradual increase and, again, a gradual decrease in tension. Re-order the set succession, placing any set at any position in the progression to further the design.

application

Dissonance factors can be applied on three distinct levels. First, there is the inherent factor of the entire set. Second is the factor related to the adjacent intervals, and last is the projected factor consisting of all internal intervals.

Let us employ these manners of arriving at dissonance factors to create a succession of three sets of different size; 3-3 (df 3 2/3), 4-Z15 (df 3 1/2), and 5-Z12 (df 3 3/5). All are very close to the same inherent factor and project a slightly increasing tension when placed in order 4-Z15, 5-Z12, 3-3.

The Comparison factors of the sets are 3-3=3 2/3, 4-Z15=3 1/2, and 5-Z15=3 3/5. All are very close to the same factor and project a slightly increasing tension when placed in order 4-Z15, 5-Z12 and 3-3.

While any order of spacing will produce the same factor as all intervals are included in calculations, their factors are refined by the appearance of the outside voices. That is, the df relating to the spacing of a given collection is equal to the inherent factor of the set minus the factor of the interval formed by the outside voices.

Therefor, set 3-3 can project df4 if the outside interval is ic3, 4 1/2, with ic4 outside, and 2 1/5 is ic1 is placed in outer voices.

Set 4-Z15 is modified by outside voices as follows:

outside interval		projected df
ic6	=	3 2/5
ic5	=	4
ic4	=	3 4/5
ic3	=	3 3/5
ic2	=	3 1/5
ic1	=	3

The possible factors of 5-Z12 are:

ic6	=	3 5/9
ic5	=	3 8/9 (two forms)
ic4	=	3 7/9
ic3	=	3 2/3
ic2	=	3 4/9
ic1	=	3 1/3

Notice that the most dissonant projected factor results if the external interval is the most consonant (lowest df) of the collection. Conversely, the most consonant projected factor results when the most dissonant interval of the collection appears as the external interval.

The projected and inherent factors allow us to compare the relative tension of different sets and their modification by outside voice (thus, the internal intervallic content.) However, the refinement of df produced by spacing is necessary to finalize the succession. As all internal, projected factors of 4-Z15 will be the same, regardless of the order in which those pc's are placed when the outside interval is, say, ic1, our earlier studies have shown that differing internal spacings produce different effective df's for each.

The following spacings all employ ic5 as the outside interval of 4-Z15. All result in a projected factor of df3, while each is perceived to present a different texture. The first exposes ic's 3,4,6 to produce a df by virtue of spacing of 3 (df's 3+2+4=9, divided by three). The next presents ic's 1(df6), 4(df2), and 2(df5), with a resultant df of 4 1/3. The df resulting from the last two spacings are easily calculated.

The use of the inherent factor informs us on the level of set. The projected factor is a function of the use of a specific interval in the outside voices, the most strongly perceived interval, and the framework for the presentation of the internal contents. The df related to the specific adjacent intervals allows for the comparison of different orderings of the same internal pc's.

Let us employ the above three sets in order of increasing inherent factors. As previously discerned, this will result in the succession of 4-Z15,
5-Z12 and 3-3. Let us refine our design to provide the most dissonant projected factor, which simply means placing the most consonant interval of
each set in the outer voices. Let the adjacent internal intervals be ordered
to expose the most consonant combinations possible.

The most consonant arrangement of outer voices employs ic5 for both
the 4n and 5n sets, and ic4 for the 3n. The examples below could occur on
any pitches. Those shown are for comparison only.

EX.70

The only choice needed to complete the last set is whether to employ pc
3 or 5. Either will result in the same set, as well as projected and spacing
factors. 4-Z15 may employ either the normal or inverted form, comprised
of pc's 1,5 or 2,8. 5-Z12 must chose between pc's 3,5,8 or 1,4,6.

EX.71

The possible spacings for 4-Z15 are shown below. In keeping with our pre-
compositional decisions, either spacing resulting in df3 may be employed.

EX.72

There are more possibilities for 5-Z12, as we must examine the effective
spacings of three internal pc's. The first is the most consonant. Only one of
the two possible collections of Pc's which complete the set with the outer
ic5 is shown. Its inversional form may be employed instead.

EX.73

In example 74, below, the sets will be placed in order of increasing set membership. Their succession in order of increasing inherent df will be deferred for completion in assn. 35, below.

The first set, 3-3, may be completed by pc3. If 4-Z15 is completed by Pc's 5,1, pc3 may progress by ic2 to either. If completed by Pc's 4,8, pc3 would progress by ic1 to pc4, or by ic5 to pc8.

EX.74

Employing Pc's 1,5 combines with the internal pc3 of 3-3 to form 3-6 (0,2,4). If Pc's 1,8 complete 4-Z15, they combine with pc3 in 3-9 (0,2,7). If 3-3 is completed by pc5, instead, a held tone results when 4-Z15 is completed by pc's 1,5, producing a very smooth connection. If pc's 4,8 are used in 4-Z15, they combine with the internal pc5 of 3-3 in an inner presentation of set 3-3. Employing these latter pc's will result in a contiguous vertical statement of 3-3 in the upper three voices of the 4n set, as well. This is the most coherent possibility, projecting 3-3 on various strong levels.

EX.75

Regardless of which form of 5-Z12 is used, normal or inversional, one common internal pc results. The first, employing pc's 6,1,4, presents no strong set re-use. The second continues a presentation of 3-3 (pc's 4,7,3 and 4,8,5). Our line now appears as follows:

EX. 76

Now let us employ the same succession of sets and internal spacing with minimal pc recurrence. As 4-Z15 contains 3-3 as a subset, we may investigate the vector of 3-3 for the T-levels which produce non-common tones. These are T's 2,5,6, shown below.

EX. 77

These forms of 3-3 may be completed in 4-Z15, as follows:

EX. 78

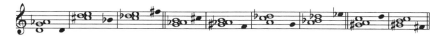

If those collections presenting a common tone with the pc's of 3-3 are discarded, the following remain possibilities, and are shown in the spacing which our design demands.

EX. 79

Examining the outer voices and their connection to pc's 2,6 (the outer voices of the first set) will refine our possibilities.

EX.80

Of the first two possibilities, that with pc3 below is preferable, as the similar motion into ic5 is by step in one voice and jump in the other, rather than both by skip in the same direction. The other possibilities show two in contrary motion being preferable to those involving similar motion of skips in both voices. Our final decision will be based on the connection of internal voicings.

EX.81

The voice-leading of the first example is too awkward, presenting ic5 in the middle voice. The second, wider scoring is better, with ic1 in the middle voice in contrary motion to the outer voices. No strong set usage occurs among the inner voices. The third example, while presenting an occurrence of parallelism between the inner and upper voices, is still a possibility as the parallelism may be mitigated by rhythmic means. We may also rely on the introduction of a new inner voice to divert attention from this defect in voice-leading. In addition, while the upper three voices of 4-Z15 combine in 3-3, the lowest two pc's of each set combine in a vertical, contrapuntal unfolding of 4-Z15 (pc's 1,2,5,7). Of the remaining possibilities, not only do none present such strong set identity, but many present "tonal" collections in the inner voices.

The two sets have employed pc's 1,2,5,6,7,8,11 which combine in set 7-19, the complement of 5-19. Only use of this latter set will allow for the completion of the progression employing totally fresh pcs. Therefor, any form of 5-Z12, our precompositionally determined set, will result in some re-use. This need not occur between the adjacent 4n and 5n sets. The latter could present all new tones in relation to the previous set, while re-introducing some pc of 3-3. This can be fulfilled by pcs 9,10,0,2,3. Again, no strong set memberships occur strictly in the middle voices. However, sets 3-2 and 3-3 result from registral association with pc11 of the previous set, and the lowest voice of the progression presents a linear unfolding of 3-3.

EX.82

Assn. 35: Complete the progression with 5-19. Be sure to analyze the contents of the set and the possibilities for internal spacings as illustrated above.

Devise a setting of the progression 4-Z 15, 5-Z 12 and 3-3. Using the same 3n and 4n sets with either of the 5n sets generated above, complete the following designs:

· the most dissonant projected and spacing factors
· the most consonant projected and spacing factors
· the most consonant projected factor with the internal pc's arranged for the most dissonant spacing.

chapter 12

MULTI-VOICE SETTINGS

recurrent set use

A given line may be accompanied throughout by a single set, or any group of sets. The three examples which follow are all settings of the first two pc's of the original line. The first two settings employ 3-2 against each pc of the original. Notice the mixture of directions and the dissimilar intervals resulting form motion in similar direction. The first employs spacings that result in df by spacing of 11/2 and 8/2. The second example employs a re-use of the same intervals of ic 2 and 3, both resulting in df 8/2.

EX.83

The next example combines pc's 11 and 2 in two different versions of 3-3, spaced for df 9/2. The first employs compound intervals, the second inversions. While all voices progress downward, each is a distinct and easily recognizable interval.

EX.84

The last example connects pc's 11,2 by way of a progression of 3-6 and 3-2. The first set has an inherent df of 12/3, the second 14/3. Set 3-6 is presented with its most consonant interval externally giving a projected factor of 10/2, while the more dissonant 3-2 presents its most dissonant interval externally, with a projected df of 8/2.

EX.85

Pc's 1,3, which accompany pc11, form 4-1 with the following pc's 0,2. The upper two voices of each set also form 4-1. Pc's 11,2 form 3-2 with either pc of the middle voice and 3-3 with the lower. The outer voices of the first result in two forms of 3-3 when combined with either of the upper two pc's of the setting of 3-2.

The following is a setting of the line in which 3-2 was chosen to occur against every pc of the original.

EX.86

Ic5 is strongly featured in the lowest line, occurring between pc's 8,3,11,6, and 2,7. It occurs once in the middle voice from pc's 8 to 1. The middle voice unfolds 3-2, pc's 9,0,11, and linked on 11 with 9,8. Its last three pc's, 1,4,5, result in 3-3. There are two instances of voice exchange. The first occurs against pc10 and the last against pc3. Both are important pitches and the similarity of spacing, coupled with the voice exchange, draws attention to their contents.

The setting of pc9 in close position is a voice cross involving all three voices. This occurs at the beginning of the second 4n sub-phrase after a held tone and, as such, will not confuse the ear. Such a motion in the middle of a fragment would present great difficulties. A variety of spacings is employed, providing a fluctuating dissonance factor.

Assn. 36: Complete settings of the line with 3-1 and 3-3.

use of multiple sets

The next setting corrects some defects of pitch occurrence of the first example and employs sets 3-2 and 3-3.

EX.87

The middle line begins with pc's 0,1 in a distinct register. The following three pc's 7,9,10 form 3-2. Pc10 progresses to pc2 which links registrally with the opening pc's of the line in 3-1, and an associated occurrence of 3-3, pc's 1,10,2.

The first three positions of the line finds 3-3 in the lower two voices, pc's 0,3,4. Pc's 11,1 link registrally to present 3-1 with the previous pc0. The low, closely spaced pc's 6,7 complete 3-3 with pc4, and 4-3 with the inclusion of pc3, registrally linked. Pc's 6,7 progress to pc's 10, which results in 3-3, and 9 to form 3-2. The motion to pc11 completes 3-1 in the lower voices. Pc's 10,11 link to 1,2. Pc1 completes 3-2 with the previous pc's and pc2 completes 3-3. The whole presents 4-1. The last pc5 combines with pc's 1,2 for a final statement of 3-3.

Assn. 37: Complete settings of the line employing 3-1 and 3-2; 3-1 and 3-3: 3-1, 3-2, 3-3.

The last setting of the line presents sets 3-1, 3-2, and 3-3 strongly, as a result of the linear progression of individual voices. The free succession of vertical sets is the result of voice leading.

EX.88

The middle line projects 3-3 (0,8,11; 8,11,7; 11,7,10), followed by 3-2 (10,1,0), and finally 3-3 (1,0,4). The bottom line consists of linked forms of 3-2 (3,4,6), 3-3 (6,5,2), 3-2 (5,2,3), 3-3 (2,3,11), (11,10,7).

Assn. 38: Construct a similar setting, forming the middle and lower voices entirely of sets 3-1, 3-2, and 3-3, allowing new sets to occur vertically as the result of voice leading. Space the sets to provide a more graceful succession of df.

refinements

Refinements of rhythm or embellishment may, of course, be applied to our three-voice settings, as in the examples below taken from the first setting of the line.

EX.89

The first example anticipates pc0, forming 3-3 with the first vertical structure. The others absorb the anomalous ic5 of the lowest voice by various
embellishments. The first connects pc's 8,3 with 6,5, forming 4-10 as a
linked succession of 3-2. In addition, these interpolated pc's form 3-3 with
the middle voice of the first vertical set and the upper pc of the second.
They also combine to form 3-5 with the upper voice of the first and middle
voice of the second trichords.

Assn. 39: Perform similar refinements by way of rhythm and embellishment on the three voice settings presented above.

The further refinement of imitation may be employed on any level – set,
shape, interval, or exact – either before or after the occurrence of the imitated shape in the original line.

EX.90

Assn. 40: Complete a three-voice setting which features imitation, of all
types, throughout in both accompanying lines.

generating a fourth voice

Four-voice settings can proceed by adding a line to our existing three-part
structure. In expanding our 3n sets to include a fourth member, 3-3 (0,1,4)
can become 4-2 (0,1,2,4) or 4-3 (0,1,3,4); 3-2 can be expanded into 4-1 or
4-3; 3-1 can become 4-1 or 4-2.

The example below places the three-voice structure above a staff on which
the pc's able to expand the three-voice structures into justifiable 4n sets are
exhibited. The last line shown on the third staff is comprised of pc's from
the pitch field shown on the middle line.

EX.91

Assn. 41: Analyze and discuss the above bass line, the 4n sets, df and inter-linear associations,especially with the upper voice.

Craft other bass lines from the given pitch field.

Generate pitch fields to expand the previous three-voice settings and construct at least two different bass lines for each setting.

A fourth voice may be added by retaining the pc's of the second and third lines, but resulting in all new voice leading between pc's. Here, the pc's of the lower lines devolve back into a generated pitch field and a pc is added to expand the field into three accompanying pc's. The resultant pitch field is re-scored to result in completely fresh lines.

EX.92

Assn. 42: Analyze the pitch field and four-voice setting completely. Discuss. Extract pc's from the lower two voices of previous examples into an expanded pitch field and re-score for new lines. Analyze the results.

Exchange the position of the lines so that the bass occurs as the tenor and again as the alto, the tenor as alto and bass, and the alto as bass and tenor. Analyze the results especially for the upper and lower voice in combination, the combined effect of soprano and alto, alto and tenor, and tenor and bass, and for any changes in df, on any level.

Consider the following:

EX.93

4.2	4.2	4.3	4.3	4.4	4.3	4.2	4.1	4.3	4.2	4.1	4.3
16	14	15	11	11	12	13	16	13	10	16	17

Notice the relatively gradual flow of df throughout the line.

This setting illustrates important considerations regarding inner lines. Unless some care is exercised, inner lines may be conceived or perceived as "filler", present merely to flesh out harmonies suggested by the dominant outer voices. Giving life to inner lines is, in many respects, the essence of counterpoint.

The alto line consists of pc's 9,0,1,8,9,1,4. Set 3-3 is first exposed as an ordered progression of ic's 3 and 1. This is followed by presentation of each ic – ic1 as pc's 8,9, and ic3 as pc's 1,4. Set 3-3 connects to pc8 by means of ic5. Both pc's of ic3 exist at T5 from the pc's of ic1 – 8,1 and 9,4. Ic4 plays a prominent role in the construction of the line, being the span of the first three pc's, the connection between the presentation of ic's 1 and 4 (8,9), and in inversion as the span from the first pc of ic1 to the last of ic3 8(9)(1)4.

A consistent logic also guides the tenor line. The first three pc's present linking ic's 4 (7,3,3,11,7,[3],11). A self contained version follows from pc6 to pc10. Ic3 is interlocked to present to last three pc's – 11,8,5.

Application of consistent logic gives inner lines life and character. Only through such means does the inner line "sing through" to the ear. This is an especially important consideration when the inner voices are not strongly independent in nature, as is the case with this setting.

The relation of each inner line to all accompanying lines also exhibits use of a considered logical choice. Notice the insistence on ic's 1 and 2 between soprano and alto, with ic3 interspersed throughout.

ic 2 2 1 3, 1 3 1 2, (4) 3 2 1

Alto and tenor combine to represent ic's 1 and 2, with the latter dominating the first half and ic1 functioning strongly in the second.

ic 2 (3) 2, 2 1 2 1, (4) 1

Alto and bass; ic (1 4 1) 2 3 2 3, 2 3

Tenor and bass; ic 1 1 3 4 2 2 2
(ic1 vs. tenor ic4 are echoed
by ic2 vs. tenor ic's 3)

Soprano and alto; ic (4) 1 2 1, 3 2 3 1 3, 1 1 2

The alto line presents 3-3 (9,0,1). Its next, pc8, combines with 3-3 to form 4-7 (0,1,4,5) which may be seen as the combination of two forms of 3-3 – 9,0,8 and 9,0,1. The return to pc9, held against the succeeding four positions of the line followed by pc1, adds no new sets.

Successive ic's 4 begin the tenor line, which ends with ic's 3. The bass line was constructed to project more and continuing registral set usage. The opening successive ic's 8 impart a definable character to the line, which continues with a preponderance of rather wide leaps. Notice the progression of intervals formed by this line in combination with the melody.

EX.94

ic3   ic2   ic3   ic4   ic1   T3   T5   T1   T1   T2   T3   ic4

The line begins with an imitation of shape usage of the original, answering the descending ic9 with a simultaneous ascending ic8. The ic1 is answered by ic2 by way of suspension, both descending. The final ascending ic9 is answered by an ascending ic8, effecting imitation modified by interval exchange. For all remaining position except the last, the lines exist a ic1. The upward ic3 (pc's 9,0) is answered by ic3 at T1, but in inversion, echoing the relation of the two lines at the outset. The next ic1 (pc8 above pc7) forms an actual progression of ic's 11 and 9, both compound. Of these couplings, the first contains the lower numbered of the pc's forming ic1 in the upper voice, while the second – bass line pc1 – is the higher numbered. The next is a parallel, with the bass voice leaping down by ic13. This pc is held while the upper voice progresses to pc5, a compound presentation of ic1 above the held pc6. Again, the pitches exchange order of higher-lower numbered pc's. This progresses to ic1 with the lower pc of the interval occurring in the original line.

The bass and tenor voices exhibit relationships throughout which indicate special and continuing emphasis on their interaction. Their opening combinations employ ic1, those in the middle portion emphasize ic's 3,4 and the ending positions employ ic2 exclusively. This construction was favored in order to echo the general sweep of the succeeding fragments of the upper line, where the first fragment relies on ic1, the second exposes contiguous ic's 3,4 and the end exhibit a sweep of ic2.

The example below extracts sets occurring between the outer voices.

EX.95

The contiguous sets occurring in the lowest line are shown in example 96.

EX.96

Registral association plays an important role in focusing strong set use among the primarily new, accidental sets.

EX.97

Strong set usage is revealed by an examination of inter-linear associations.

EX.98

There is much use of voice exchange and held tones in this setting, which affects a general slowing of the motion. Notice the voice exchange on pc10 between tenor and bass voices, resulting from an apparent – but greatly disguised – simultaneous downward leap of ic's 8 and 9. The following example charts these successive pitch recurrences.

EX.99

As held pitches impress the ear rather strongly, these pc's may tend to associate by motion (oblique) much as the manner in which wide jumps of various ic's tend to be heard as somehow related. The sets resulting from pc's in oblique motion agree strongly with controlling sets. In the second position 3-3 occurs. The next placement adds pc1, giving a form of 3-2 in the upper voices, with the whole projecting 4-3. The voice exchange on pc1 is followed by held pc's 9,10 to form 3-3. Later, held pc's 8,6 appear against the longest held pc9 to form 3-2. Pc8 combined with pc9 and the previous voice-exchanged pc10 result in 3-1, while pc's 10,9 combine with pc6 in 3-3. Pc's 6,8 are followed by 4,5, forming 3-1 (4,5,6), 3-3 (8,4,5), and 3-2 (5,6,8). The last held pc7 combines with pc's 4,5 in 3-2.

Assn. 43: Construct a four-voice setting in which held tones are featured by design to combine in either strongly presented sets, or to introduce new sets not found contiguously.

chapter 13

FANTASIA FOR STRING QUARTET

Our multi-voice composition will be a fantasia for string quartet. The fantasia is a free variation form, proceeding primarily from a contrapuntal framework. A mixture of imitation, free counterpoint, figuration and development should be employed.

The fantasia again proceeds from a fully crafted line, guided and controlled by some combination of set, shape, intervallic and rhythmic factors. Succeeding sections may employ the entire line, a specific fragment or a variety of fragments, in any order. All varied usages of materials may appear in the same section, succeeding one another freely or occurring simultaneously. The original line may be represented by an abstraction of some procedure of the line. For instance, the opening of the original line used throughout this text could be abstracted as progression or combination of a specific interval by ic1.

Each succeeding section may be discrete, featuring a distinct beginning and end, or continuous, proceeding by elision or transition. Each may consist purely of imitation, free counterpoint, figuration or development. A mixture of various approaches may be featured, succeeding one another or combining in any order for any length of time.

The sections should each portray a distinct character. That character is a reflection of the procedures to which they are subjected. Rhythm, set, shape, tessitura and instrumental color, spacing and usage are all aspects to consider in defining the character of a section. All may be very narrowly defined or consist of any number of dissimilar or related elements, to be employed in various combinations and successions.

The fantasia allows for free creative rein. Any and all procedures developed for single – and multi-voice writing may be imaginatively employed, on materials derived from or related to generating or controlling factors. In general, the presentation of materials should be so structured and unfolded as to expose character, controlling factors, procedures, and materials, subjecting them to a breaking apart, re-working, and re-association.

The following rather extended example will serve to illustrated the great freedom of the formal procedures of the fantasia.

A variety of textures is employed, exposing from one to all four instruments, combining on various numbers of simultaneous pitch combinations from all instruments on a single unison pc to the final 8n sonority.

Here, the fluctuation is fairly rapid. Succeeding sections or phrases may continue or vary this pace. A single texture of any number of voices may continue for relatively long periods of time.

The various registers have been assigned discrete, if overlapping functions. The middle register is primarily employed for unison or closely positioned collections. The lowest registers project melodic material, which also occurs fragmented in the upper registers. Homophonic set progressions are restricted to the highest register. While such registrally defined occurrences may continue to be a factor of the character of this or succeeding sections, any of the registers may undergo constant change.

EX. 100

Rhythm is carefully considered and employed. The opening figure of a sixteenth-note pick-up to a longer value continues throughout the section. The longer value justifies the occurrence of held pc's against which a line in shorter values may occur. Sixteenth-note triplets then grow out of the pick-up figure, with the violin I eighth-note, pc5, acting as a pick-up to the following pc6.

Eighth notes then proceed in the highest register, first as a homophonic statement of the set employed to accompany the cello line sixteenth-note triplets. The cello line ends with a pickup and longer value on pc10, followed by a similar figure in viola as a unison pick-up tied to a longer value, rather than attacked. The upper register eighth-notes proceeding from this point continue the pick-up figure.

Notice the various positions within the measure on which the figure re-curs.

All shapes, sets intervallic usages are derived from the germinal line. The opening pc's of the line are exactly those of the original. Pc11 is stated in unison and introduces the prime rhythmic figure. Pc2 proceeds to pc1 in violin II, exactly as in the original, with the upper pc10 occurring simultaneously. The following pc's of the original, pc's 9,0, occur in cello and violin I, respectively, against the held pc1.

Set 3-3 is strongly featured, as shown in example 101.

EX.101

The opening pc11 combines registrally with the opening pc's of the cello to form 3-2 (11,9,8). This set has also occurred from pc11 to the violin II pc's 2,1 and between violin II's pc1 and pc's 10,0 of violin I. This progression from forms of 3-2 to 3-3 imitates the opening sets of the original line. The cello line imitates first the set content of 3-2, progressing to an exact imitation of the shape of 3-3.

Violin I presents the accidental set of 3-6 (10,0,2). This combines with the cello to project the intervallic succession of ic's 1,4,3, the interval content of 3-3. Pc's 0,2 of the upper line combine with the held pc1 of violin II to form set 3-1, which is featured in the following fragment beginning on the unison (11,0,10), and in combination between cello and violin I (pc's 10,9,8). The violin I line presents an intervallically and registrally transformed imitation of 3-3 in two versions, pc's 0,9,8 and 9,8,5. Pc's 10 (vc) and 0,9,8 (vln I) combine in 4-2.

The succeeding fragment expands 3-3 into 4-3; pc's 2,5,6 + pc3 and 3,7,4,6. Violin I presents a linear occurrence of 3-1 (5,4,6). A registral occurrence of 3-2 results from viola pc3 and violin pc's 5,6 and 4,6. These last pc's proceed in the same voice to pc8, exposing a re-use of the accidental 3-6. The entire violin line of pc's 5,6,4,8 combines to form 4-2.

This set also occurs in the middle voice (via) of the following homophonic statement of 3-3 in the upper three voices, as pc's 5,8,9,7,10,11, and 9,0,1. The outer ic's of this progression imitate the ic's occurring on the second beat in ms.2 in violins. Both violins project 3-3 horizontally.

EX.102

The cello line in ms.4 presents sets 3-1, 3-2, and 3-3 in contiguously linked succession. Its upper pc's 8,11,10 form 32. Stressed pc's are 6 (or 7), 8, and

10, forming 3-6 and/or 3-2, combining in 4-2. In combination with the upper three voices, the following sets are found.

EX.103

In ms.4, the viola double-stops pc's 7,9 and 7,8 form 3-2 with cello pc10, and 3-2 and 3-1 with violin II pc6. Pc's 6,7 double stop in violin II combines with pc10 in 3-3. Pc11 in the highest voice completes 6-1, the set which exists as the first and second half of the original line. The violin I double-stop, pc's 9,11 combines with pc10 in cello in 3-1, with 7,8 in viola in 42, and with 6,7 in violin II in 4-11 (0,1,3,5; 3-2 + 3-6).

Pc1 in violin II occurs linked to pc's 9,11 to project 3-6. Pc's 11,1 are succeeded by 0,3 = 4-2 (3-3 + 3-2). Set 4-11 recurs as the result of the progression of pc's 0,3 to 2,10. Violin II projects 3-1 in imitation of earlier occurrences, and proceeds to pc11 to complete 4-1. The entire collection consists of 11,1,0,3,2,10 = 6-1.

The upper register of the violin I line in ms.5 projects a horizontal occurrence of 3-4 (11,3,10 = 10,1,5). This set is also formed at the bar-line with pc's 3,10 (vln I) and pc2 (vln II). The first appearance of this collection was on the second beat of ms.2, where it occurred as an accidental set by virtue of the held pc1. Notice the re-use of this and other accidental sets, notably 3-6, 4-11 elevating them to sets of local-level importance.

The two-voice presentation of violins in mss. 5,6 is succeeded by a return to a texture of three upper voices, projecting set 3-2 (10,11,1; 11,0,2), 3-3 (8,11,0), and 3-6 (8,10,0). Violin I proceeds from pc1 to pc's 10,11 = 3-2. The following example charts sets occurring between the voices, explaining specific pitch choice.

EX.104

Again, this three-voice progression serves to accompany a melodic state-ment in the cello, an exact use of the third through eighth pitches of the original line, reshaped first to imitate the shape of the opening 4n fragment of the original, but employing the repetition of the opening pick-up figure in the lower register. This is followed by an exact repetition of shape and content of the original line. The cello line combines with the upper voices to project the following 4n sets:

EX.105

4.2 4.1   4.3   4.2

The cello and viola combine in 3-1 (7,8,9) with 7,9 being held to combine with pc's 5,8 in the violins to form 4-2. The viola pc9 completes 3-2 hori-zontally (10,0,9).

The last 4n fragment of the original occurs in violin II, ms.9. The set occurrences of the violins in mss. 9,1,0 are shown below.

EX.106

3.3   3.6   3.1   3.2
                                     3.3

The first ic3 (pc's 5,8) combines with the lower voices in 4-2 (7,9,5,8) and 4-4 (4,7,8,9). Cello and violins sustain 3-3 (4,7,8) against the viola figure on 4-3 (6,10,9,5), shaped to imitate the original opening 4n fragment. Pc's 4,7,8 combine with the individual pc's of the viola to form 4-2 (4,6,7,8), 4-12 (4,7,8,10; 3-3 + 3-2), and 4-3 (4,5,7,8). The viola then quotes the opening 4n fragment, varied only by rhythm. This statement combines with the violins to produce the following:

EX.107

3.12 3.4   3.8 3.4   3.6   3.3   3.3   3.1   3.2
(ic4 max)

Pc's 10,9 are held against the horizontal unfolding of 3-2 in violin II to produce 3-2 (10,0,9) and 3-3 (10,1,9). The last sonority, a cluster of 8n, produces
associations as follows: ic2 (0,2) progresses outward by half-step to ic4 (11,3).
These ic's suggest the previous intervallic succession resulting in 3-6, but
combine in 4-3. The following ic2, consisting of pc's 6,8, is succeeded by
ic4 (0,8, 2,6) and pc's 11 ,3, by ic3 (3,6,11,8), presenting the interval content
of 4-3 vertically and in progression. The last two pc's complete 8-8, an
intersection of 3-1 and 5-1, with the former clustered in vla/vc (6,7,8) and
the latter in close position above.

An analysis of procedures shows that the section opens with an occurrence of the original opening 4n fragment at pitch, but differentiated by
rhythm, register and by virtue of simultaneous occurrence. This is followed by the presentation of new materials in the upper voices acting as
accompaniment to an abridged imitation in the cello. The opening unison
is reprised and expanded, dove-tailing into a statement in violin I which
imitates the opening ensemble statement. The following vln I/vla pc's re-
work the new material presented in violins in ms.2. Another re-working of
this material combines in a three-voice statement of the important set 3-3
as accompaniment, against a cello line which expands and transforms the
melodic shapes presented so far. This flows into an expanded recurrence
of the previous unison statement.

A duet of violins follows which presents an important intervallic succession, exposed in order to prepare the following three-voice succession.
Again, this accompanies a cello statement which restates a rather large
number of pitches of the original line. Now, violin II quotes from the original while the active viola, fashioned after the shape of the first and last 4n
segments of the original, proceeds as a contrapuntal embellishment. This is
followed by a quote of the opening 4n exactly at pitch. The section ends on
a dense cluster which has developed from the opening unison statement.

The various shapes and materials connect from one appearance to the
next by virtue of register, rhythmic shape, instrumentation and pitch content. The first figure returns at the bar-line leading to ms.3, expanded to
include half-step motion to either side of the opening unison pitch. This
development is prompted by the intervening material which employs the
opening rhythmic figure to present ic1. The ic2 occurs as an echo of the
string of ic's 2 in violin I, ms.2. Its next entrance is in cello, ms.4. Here,
entrances are offset rhythmically and again is expanded to present 3-2 in
vc/vla. Its last occurrence is as the cluster sonority which ends the section.

EX.108

The accompaniment figure in upper voices begins in violins in ms.2. This is momentarily elevated to a surface-level statement in violin I and viola, immediately dove-tailing into an accompaniment to the cello. It occurs next in violins as primary material, allowing relationships to form undistracted by other materials, as in ms.3. Again, it moves immediately to a background level accompaniment figure. Its last presentation in mss. 9,10 expands its influence into cello and allows for internal movement as a development of its primarily background existence.

EX.109

Notice the sets formed by violins in highest register.

EX.110

The last shape is that which imitates the activity of the original line. This occurs first in cello, followed by a fragmentary rhythmic statement in

violin I. This latter connects in 3-3, not only with the previous and succeeding tones in violin I, but also with the previous cello pc. Its next two
occurrences are in cello and finally in viola.

EX.111

part 3
on-going variation: free counterpoint

chapter 14

DYADIC GENERATION

Finally, we will undertake free counterpoint, with an eye to a large-scale composition employing on-going variation. Such a composition may proceed form a variety of approaches. Materials may be developed by some guided concept from which motive, primary and background levels of activity and set content may be derived. A motive may be developed and expanded into a series of materials. Uncritically collected materials may be employed from which motive, materials, and procedures may be developed. In on-going variation, all of the above procedures figure importantly.

In all, the procedures aim at providing a constant texture of some generative set or group of sets which, in turn, generates a more complex texture of varied surface characteristics. While a given fragment or larger line may be employed to assure some continuity, our aim in free counterpoint is to produce a directed flow of continually transformed materials. These materials will exhibit all developmental procedures and variation techniques. Their succession, while strongly structured through pitch choice, set usage, imitation, et al, will result in a seemingly free association of ideas.

An interplay of surface, middle and background levels is also a factor of on-going variations. A figure which emerges first from purely local-level voice-leading may be elevated to a middle or even surface-level occurrence. Figures that were featured prominently may, conversely, recede into the background.

As in earlier procedures, some pre-compositional intentions must be defined; namely, the generative set, the method of unfolding the set and generating associative pitches, the number of voices to be employed, the character and activity of the voices. We will continue in our use of 3-2 as the generative set and will present its dyadic possibilities as the unfolding of the underlying structure of the phrase. The dyads will be used to generate pitches inter-associated in the set, but the pitches generated need not be contiguous partial or complete statements of the set. Instead, they may provide intervals and sets on the local level which are dissimilar to the generating set and each other.

The dyadic possibilities of 3-2 are ic's 1,2,3. This is a fairly elegant order as it stands, imposing a decreasing level of tension. As our phrase will be designed to be an opening statement and, therefor, rather short and self-contained, the underlying structure will benefit from some such relatively simple unfolding. More active or dense later sections may explore more complex relationships.

Let the opening ic1 be formed of pc's 2,1. These can be employed as 0,1 of the prime form of 3-2 or as 2,3 of the inversion. Pc's 1,2 as 0,1, is completed in 3-2 by pc4; as 2,3 it is completed by pc11. These new pc's combine to form ic5(7), an interval not found in 3-2. If we connect these two pc's, placing them together by means of articulation, we might suggest that all four pc's should be heard as a single entity – set 4-10 (0,2,3,5; pc's 11,1,2,4). In order to state the supremacy of 3-2 most strongly, it may prove wise to provide a break between the occurrences of pc's 4,11, leaving the contiguous occurrence of this interval until later in the piece when its existence as a surface level manifestation of the unfolding of 3-2 is more clearly evident.

EX.112

Next, we must generate the dyad ic2, the middle interval of our progression. We may proceed form a number of approaches. One might be to explore other possible associations of 3-2 by using each first-level pitch of ic5 and each of the pc's of the background structure singly. Combining pc's 4,1 suggests pc's 2,3 to complete the next generation. Pc2 is already present, pc3 remains a possibility. Combining pc's 4,2 suggests pc1 (already present) and pc5. Pc's 11,2 yield only pc10, new, and pc's 11,2 gives pc1. Either collection of tones – pc's 3,4 or 10,0 – fulfill the intervallic needs of our design to feature ic2 at this point. Let us explore scoring these in conjunction with the opening ic1 consisting of pc's 2,1.

The possible scorings are as follows:

EX.113

All four scorings are different unfoldings of 4-2. This relates strongly to 3-2, as an expansion. The first and third versions are inversionally related, as are the second and fourth. In the first mentioned inversional group, one tone progresses by ic1 and the other by ic4. In the alternating settings, the progressions are ic's 3,2. On the basis of just this much information, either the second or fourth provide a more elegant solution as they progress by intervals of 3-2 not yet occurring in the background level. We now have two possible progressions.

EX.114

The tones of the lower two voices could be employed to suggest following pc's which may complete 3-2. The example below charts this procedure. Pc's already present appear in parentheses.

EX.115

Only pc's 0,6 are fresh tones. The use of pc0 presents some difficulties. First, neither pc's 11 or 0 will continue the maximal use of 3-2 in combination with pc's 3,5. Pc11 can only generate 3-2 by progressing from pc0 to pc9; pc0 could combine with pc3 in a form of 3-2, but both tones needed to complete the set, pc's 1,2, are already present. If pc9 is used to follow pc0, we will reinforce a surface level of 3-2 and a structural level of 3-8, appearing in two versions, pc's 11,3,5 and 3,5,9. This is the reverse of our pre-compositional intent to provide maximal usage of 3-2 in relation to the background interval against surface disparity.

An investigation of the second possible scoring may solve our difficulties. There are some intriguing factors, here. The upper pc11 forms 3-2 with the middle voice pc's 1,10 and with the lowest voice pc's 2,0. A generation similar to the one provided in example 115 will show that only pc's 3,9 were generated as new possible pc's. Only pc9 provides a statement of 3-2 with the background dyad. However, use of this pc in the upper voice presents registral difficulties. If the pc's are kept in their present positions we could not proceed from pc11 to pc9 step-wise, as parallel ic's 3 would result between the outer voices. The upper line would have to be revised into one of the following shapes.

EX.116

While the first and fourth re-scorings emphasize the ic's 5(7) surrounding pc4 very nicely, the first reaches climax in a new register in a line of ever increasing leaps. Climax itself is no difficulty: there must be one somewhere in the phrase. Opening a new register so drastically does present problems, however. To this point, we have employed rather close movement, using only ic's 2,3,7. The re-scorings include ic's 10,14.

The second, fourth, and fifth re-scorings would result in a crossed voice. This need create no special problems where instrumental color and an offset attack can point out the identity of pc9 as a member of the upper, melodic, line. However, the overall structure and inter-relationship may still be obscured.

A different solution would be to jump the lower voices upward, disguising the parallel ic's 3 through registral shift. Here we open no new register, or at least not drastically, but the voice cross will still occur. In fact, it must occur or all voices will be progressing by rather large jumps, a useful procedure where discontinuity is a facet of the pre-compositional intent. But there is a hidden parallel ic10 from pc's 1 to 0 and 11 to 10 (see ex.117). Color and rhythm may combine to break the association, but let us explore a further possibility.

EX.117

Instead of generating the lower voices first, let us generate possible surface level pc's to see if they can inform the process. So far, we have a vertical interval of ic1(11) and a horizontal interval of ic5(7). Perhaps these intervals can be featured on the surface, thus adding strength to their juxtaposition.

From pc11, let us progress by ic's 1 and 5 in all possible permutations.

EX.118

The greater majority of the possibilities will not fulfill our design, which calls for both tones to be part of interlocking sets 3-2, associating with ic2 below. Those with ic5 or 6 immediately following pc11 are therefor excluded. So are those which include an already present tone. Only those with ic4 can be combined in two forms of 3-2 with the lower ic2. This leaves only the last possibility generated - pc's11,10,6.

Pc6 extends the opening ic7. Pc10, in conjunction with the preceding pc's 4,11 gives a surface set of 3-5.

Only one possible ic2 will combine with pc's 10,6 to provide interlocking forms of 3-2, namely pc's 7,9. Let us now examine the relationships between our first background interval of pc's 2,1 and ic2 comprised of pc's 7,9 to see if any relationship exists which further either our background structure or surface level occurrences.

The four pc's of the background combine in 4-16 (0,1,5,7; pc's 7,9,1,2). This is exactly the set formed by the four surface level pc's 4,6,10,11. By scoring pc7 at bottom and pc9 above, a lower progression of ic5 occurs to balance the same interval in the upper voice (pc's 4,11), and ic4 occurs in the middle voice the same interval which occurs between the new pc's of the upper line. In addition, set 3-5 (0,1,6), first found in the upper line, lies embedded in the lower voices (pc's 7,1,2) as does the string of ic's 5 (pc's 7,2,9).

EX.119

The last grouping of our phrase is the least problematic. We can disregard all pc's used so far and see which possible occurrences of ic3 exist in the unused tones. Only pc's 0,3,5,8 are left unused at this point. Pc's 5,8 would have to be combined with pc's 6,7 to complete our design. While this is a distinct possibility it defeats our basic design in several ways. First, it would mean suspending motion in the outer voices, as the pc's needed would have to be held from their immediately preceding placement. This would be heard as an insistence on their importance as background structure, providing a de facto progression of ic's 1,2,1, first presented in contiguous lower voices and finally as held non-contiguous outer voices. Finally, it would force the middle voice into a melodic statement of the interval we had chosen as background structure. To this point, melodic statements have presented only local level pitch choice.

The last possibility is to employ pc's 0,3, which could only be completed in 3-2 by pc's 1,2. That these pc's opened the presentation of the lower line need not deter us. Their previous use associated these pc's together, making their re-appearance an invariant use of the dyad. There is also a strong feeling of closure produced not only by the invariant pc's, but their use first as background and finally as surface.

These pc's, of course, form 3-2 with both opening pc's 4 and 7. They also form a set of local importance with both pc's 6,10; set 3-4 (0,1,5) – which first appeared as pc's 11,10,6 and here as 1,2,6. This same set occurs in the lowest voice – pc's 2,3,7.

There are some considerations attending these final pitches. First, they must occur in the order 2,1. The previous pc's 10,6 would form an F# major triad with pc1. Pc2 forms an augmented triad. Placed in this order, a descending ic1 results. A similar appearance of the interval occurred from pc11 to pc10. In order that some freedom of the unfolding line be retained, it might be best to provide each occurrence with different rhythm and/or stress to keep a motivic association from occurring. Finally, any following pitch choice should include the unused pc's 5,8.

However it is scored, some interesting relations surface. Pc's 11,10,2,1 in the upper line form an intersection of 3-2, associated registrally, by means not previously employed – ic1+ ic1 at T3. Coincidentally, the resultant 4n set (pc's 10,11,12 = 4-3, 0,1,3,4) contains interlocking forms of 3-3. This is the set featured in the middle voice as pc's 1,9,0.

The final appearance of the line and its full analysis is shown in example 120.

EX.120

Assn. 44: Use a single set, guided by a pre-conceived progression of melodic and accompaniment ic's, to produce a phrase consisting of three to six chordal structures in 3 or 4 voices.

chapter 15

MOTIVIC USAGE

<u>motivic extraction</u>

A number of motives may be developed from materials generated by procedures discussed in previous chapters. The simplest would be extraction
of portions of the line.

EX.121

3.5   3.4   4.16   4.19   3.4   3.3   3.4

The first series of examples above breaks the line of the upper voice generated in the previous chapter into groupings each of which exhibits a distinct
character by virtue of pitch-intervallic content. Their shapes are similar, a
factor which may be exploited in ensuing sections. The last two examples
are simply the middle and lower voices of the phrase.

All fragments employ ic1, most contiguously, all but one descending. This,
too, may be featured strongly throughout a work based on this phrase. Any
of the motives may be employed melodically in one voice, contrapuntally
in two (or more) voices, or occur vertically in chordal usage. Of course, set
3-2 may occur in any of the above stated manners, as its importance to the
piece has already been asserted.

Each combination of two voices could be mined for shape, interval or set
content, and employed as motive. The first line of examples below combines
materials taken from the upper and middle voices. The middle line is drawn
from the outer voices. The last line combines pc's of the lower two voices.

EX.122

3.7   4.2   4.4   3.3   3.2   3.1   3.1

3.7   3.3   3.3   4.7   3.4   3.4   3.1

3.5 3.4 3.8 3.9 3.8 3.7

Example 123, below, employs several fragments in various usages; melodic, contrapuntal, and chordal.

EX.123

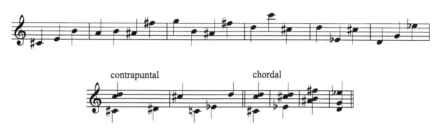

contrapuntal   chordal

Assn. 45: Extract motives from the progression in the preceding chapter. Re-figure the motives melodically, contrapuntally, and harmonically. Suggest an order for their appearance based on melodic or contrapuntal motion and/or set. Provide short examples which connect motives in the assigned order. Be sure to consider the possible connection of motives of different types of activity.

set association

The extracted motives exhibit a great variety of sets. It is necessary to absorb the variety of the extracted sets into the overall governing set in order to provide a cogent presentation and textural continuity. This is a fairly simple procedure based on contrapuntal activity. The example below illustrates the expansion of 3-2 into 3-4, the set of the bass line, and its movement back into 3-2. An example of melodic and chordal transformation is also given.

EX.124

contrapuntal melodic 3.2 3.4 harmonic

3.2 3.4 3.4 (3.3) 3.2 3.2 (3.3) 3.2 3.2 3.4 3.2

3.4 3.4

4.5

Assn. 46: Employ any motive which forms a set other than 3-2 in melodic, contrapuntal and harmonic progression with any other motive, as in the above examples.

Each of the previous examples employs a specific device to further heighten internal logic. The first proceeds primarily by ic2 in all voices. The insistence on a specific interval to generate motion provides a constant texture or character to the lines, and confers identity in much the same way as does imitation. The second (melodic) example presents registrally differentiated sets which support the transformation and association of sets: 3-3 below expanded to 4-5 (0,1,4,5 = 0,1,4 + 1,4,5) to 3-4. The last presents 3-3 as the inner line and 3-4 as the bass. In addition, 3-3 occurs as the upper voices of the last two chords. Pc's 8,7 of the middle voice are completed in 3-4 by pc3 of the second chord. Pc6 of the lower voice forms 3-4 with the following ic5 – pc's 2,7. 3-2 occurs as the lowest voice of the second chord and the lowest two pc's of the last. There are also several occurrences of 3-1, 3-6, and 3-8.

The upper voices combine to form 4-11 (3,5,7,8 = 3-2 + 3-6) and 3-3. The lower voices present 4-5 (2,6,7,8) which contains 3-1, 3-4, and 3-8 as subsets. The outer voices combine in 4-1 and 3-1. All the sets are related to 3-2 as supersets, elided subsets of supersets, or as intervallic expansions.

Assn. 47: Re-work assignment 46 to employ first a single intervallic progression and then registral or linear associations which exhibit relationship with 3-2.

The use of a motive in a single voice can provide more strength to other voices involved in a progression around a set of local importance.

EX.125

3.2   3.6   3.4   3.3 3.2   3.2   3.8 3.2 3.6 3.2

Notice set 3-2 in the middle voice of the first example above. The second presents 3-4 strongly, with associated sets 3-3 and 3-5 also occurring in linear unfolding in middle and lower voices, respectively.

Assn. 48: Employ a motive to guide a progression of dissimilar set content centering around 3-2. Let the accompanying lines exhibit important or related sets, a motive, or its transformation.

expanded motivic usage

A piece may proceed from a motive, from which materials may be derived by extraction or expansion. The motive itself need not consist wholly or in part of the controlling set. The motive may exist in one or several registers, be constructed of a single interval or a group of intervals, and may employ any rhythmic shape. The flourish below presents 3-3, 3-2, 3-3, 3-3, contiguously. Extended internal relationships are shown.

EX.126

This is a fairly simple manner in which to proceed and should be easily understood by this point as, in effect, we have employed motives (fragments of larger lines) as the generating material for all procedures throughout this text. In example 127, the generation of the middle voice is shown to be a completion of the flourish into a chromatic set. These pc's combine in a linear statement of 3-3. The first vertical interval, ic13 consisting of pc's 10,11, form 3-2 with the succeeding pc1 and 3-3 with pc2. The second icl forms 3-2 with the preceding pc11 and 3-2 with pc10. Pc1 is held beneath pc3 to expose 3-1. With pc's 3,0 above, 3-2 is formed, followed again by 3-1. Pc's 0,11 above form 3-2 with the lower pc9, as do pc's 11,8.

EX.127

The lowest voice in the example 128 was crafted to expose 3-1, 3-2 and 3-3 horizontally, and 3-3 with pc1 above and at the ending vertically.

EX.128

derivation of the motive

At times, a larger or shorter fragment may come to mind, unbidden and uncritically constructed, that captures your compositional fancy. It may be a representation of a specific activity, shape or progression, or even of instrumental usage. In order to employ such materials, an analysis must be performed to identify contents and fragments, and to suggest procedures for further use.

Example 129, below, was constructed entirely of vertical combinations of ic's 2,3,4. Ic1 occurs horizontally in the upper voice on pc's 10,9 and in the lower voice from the opening pc's 0,1 and later on 7,8. Two occurrences of ic5 are presented in the upper line, from pc's 4,11 and 9,4. Otherwise, both lines consist of ic's 2,3 with one occurrence of ic4. No real effort was made to suggest either local or governing levels of set usage.

EX.129

The upper line consists of set 3-7, with pc2 occurring on either side of the melodic ic5, exposing the entire intervallic content of the set – ic's 2,5,3. This is followed by a short pc10 forming a very transitory 3-3, extended into 3-4 and 4-4 by the equally short pc9. Pc4 which follows, combines with pc's 9,10 in 3-5 (0,1,6). The last apparent "A major" chord (3-11) is purely accidental in nature but must be investigated carefully, lest the rather free succession of (tonally) non-functional consonances be inadvertently employed to enforce "key feeling".

Combining with the previous pc10, 3-11 expands into 4-18 (0,1,4,7), a rather consonant set. Expanded to include pc2, this set becomes 5-Z 18 (0,1,4,5,7). Notice that this set combines 3-3 and 3-2 around the central pc4 (in prime form). As luck would have it, there is a registral association of these sets dovetailing on the final pc1 which holds the central position in this unfolding of the set – 9,10,1,2,4 – with 3-2 occurring above and 3-3 below pc1.

The accompanying lower line arguably dispels the feeling of movement to A, but combines with the last two upper pc's in "c#m7". Either analysis suggests that the last tones should be approached with care, perhaps revising or expanding to generate pc's which may mitigate any feeling of tonal collection. The lower line contains a symmetrical presentation of inversionally related forms of 3-2 (or 4-11 – 0,1,3,5 – linked on pc's 3,5). Pc's 1,3,5,7 present a string of ic's 2. The last three tones interlock with 3-2 on ic1 to form 3-3. The total set of the last 4n fragment presents 4-12 (0,2,3,6).

While we have catalogued melodic shape and sets for the upper line, our analysis is incomplete without an examination of the contrapuntal progression and its resultant shapes. The opening ic2 progresses to ic3, followed by an inversional occurrence of ic4. Both lines progress by ever-wider intervals – the bottom by ic1 against ic2 above, followed by ic2 below, suggesting a linear relation between vertical and horizontal intervals. Ic2 below accompanies the upward jump of ic5. The next progression places ic3 above ic2 to form a vertical ic3. The first contrary motion of the fragment proceeds by ic4 over ic2, and then by oblique motion of ic1 to form a vertical progression of ic's 3,2 to complete an extended palindrome of vertical ic's – 1,2,2,2,1. This further suggests the possibility of the lower line re-working materials or procedures of vertical occurrences.

Vertical appearances of ic's 2,4,2 progress by way of ic5 over ic1 and ic3 over 3. In all, the vertical and horizontal ic's appear as follows (ex. 130), with vertically-occurring ic's placed above and horizontal ic's of the upper and lower lines placed in respective order, below.

EX.130

The 4n sets produced are 4-2, 4-11 (11,1,3,4), 4-12 (11,2,3,5), 4-26 (2,5,7,10), 4-10 (4,7,8,9) and 4-26 (8,11,1,4). No apparent logic exists on the level of set which could be exploited for development. However, the manner in which each dyad progresses to the next reveals an occurrence which may be elevated to employment as a procedure. Notice that the opening vertical ic's

2,3 recur in the lower and upper voices respectively of the third and fourth dyads. If pc's 10,9 in the upper voice, and the accompanying pc7 are seen as an upbeat to the following ic4 (pc's 8,4), the same progression is evident, this time with ic2 above ic3. Notice, also, that each two-dyad progression consists of interlocking occurrences of 3-2 and 3-3: pc's 3,11,2 and 3,5,2; pc's 5,2,4 and 5,8,4. The dyads are so arranged to present a symmetrical progression of ic's 4,3,4. These dyads combine to form 6-Z42 (2,3,4,5,8,11) which contains several versions of 3-2 and 3-3.

EX.131

A complete analysis of 3n sets reveals some interesting set usage.

EX.132

All of the sets extracted have at least one surface appearance of contiguous pc's in either upper or lower voice. Choosing to feature any of these sets effectively elevates the occurrence of the set between the voices to a surface level presentation. Any and/or all of these recurrent sets or dyads may be exploited in discrete sections, or in any order or combination. All of the techniques previously developed may be employed.

The line receives its identity by its insistence on vertical ic's 3 and 4, while the succession of pc's generally relies on ic's 1,4. No strong set identity emerges on the surface. Instead, a fairly diverse group of set possibilities exists. Therefor, the line has a somewhat amorphous quality, making it well suited for use either as an introduction or transition. The body of the section which follows will function to define the aspects of the line which are of importance, through contrapuntal and developmental variation techniques.

As a discrete section of a piece may have an introduction, perhaps performing the role of transition, so does a piece as a whole. This may be thought of as an exposition. In on-going variation, the exposition may be presented in any manner, whether as a fully formed and strongly organized statement of line, motive and set, or as a statement of fragments more-or-less strongly presented or amorphous. In the extended example which follows, the latter approach was taken.

EX.133

analysis

First, a rather nebulous succession of sets was abstracted from the materials.

EX.134

This sub-phrase performs several functions. First, it exposes a rather simple development of a specific rhythmic figure of eighth and dotted quarter as a rhythmic repetition. Its retrograde, dotted quarter and eighth, is next employed, this time on separate ic's, with pc's 4,1 occurring as an eighth note one-and-a-half quarters after the attack of the half-note ic2. These are the pc's of the opening line subjected first to octave displacement and then inversion. Next the retrograde figure is employed in diminution, again for the introduction of new pc's 3,7.

The intervallic succession of ic's 2,3,4 is introduced, as well as combinations of pc's which justify particular set usage. Spacing the opening ic2 as a compound interval and the following ic3 in inversion produces a registral occurrence of ic2, and was chosen in order to feature the re-use of the opening interval, in an inter-linear statement. This, in turn, justifies any subsequent use of 3-6, which is strongly featured in the lower voice of the original materials. The linking ic's could have been attacked simultaneously, but were specifically employed in oblique entrances, as the ear hears outside pc's best, intervals formed with outside pc's, and among adjacent pc's strongly. This use of staggered entrances allows for focus on both opening pc's (upper and lower), and accentuates the recurrence of ic2 in adjacent inner pc's. Placing pc1 above the other pc's produces an upper occurrence of 3-2. The outside pc's of the first and second sonorities projects 3-1. Pc4 will impress the ear by virtue of its close position with pc2 in ic2, an interval that does not blend as well as a consonant interval would, and also because it is a new pc in the total collection. In combination with the outside voices, 3-3 is justified. The entire collection is 4-2, containing subsets 3-1, 3-2, and 3-3.

The following ic4(8), comprised of pc's 3,7 presents 3-1 as the result of the upper pc's of each ic (pc's 2,1,3), featuring ic2 first simultaneously and then in the upper voice as a progression. Pc7 combines with the previously heard pc4 and the upper voice to project 3-3. This is, of course, an introduction of the progression of the original line of ic's 8,9,8, where the upper and lower voices progress alternately by ic's 2,3. The entire 6n set is 6-Z36 (0,1,2,3,4,7), with subsets of 3-1, 3-2, 3-2; 4-1, 4-2, 4-3, 4-7 (0,1,4,5 = 3-3 + 3-3) [0,1,4 + 1,4,5] readily apparent.

The opening succession of ic's is balanced by a melodic statement with no accompaniment, contrasting the opening chordal statement with no apparent melody. This allows the exposed presentation of important ic's, sets and shapes to refine the perception of the previous chordal statement.

The pc's already used are 0,1,2,3,4,7. Their complement is pc's 5,6,8,9,10,11, which forms set 6-Z3. This set, obviously, shares its vector with 6-Z36. 6-Z3 will be used to project the melodic, balancing phrase on the level of pitch.

The three examples below are all unfoldings of the pc's of 6-Z3, each with its own intervallic and rhythmic shape.

EX.135

The first would succeed the last intervallic statement of the opening chordal structure of pc's 3,7 in a manner similar to the succession of pc's 4,1 and 7,3, but by ic's 1,2 instead of ic's 2,3. It extends the importance of ic2, forming 3-6 in the upper voice and 3-3 in the lower.

EX.136

The movement to pc9 presents a new compound interval to complete a contiguous statement of 3-3 (pc's 5,8,9). The following pc11 completes 3-2 (pc's 8,9,11). The registral association of the opening pc5 and following pc's

9,11 combines in set 3-8, an expansion of 3-6: 0,2,4 ic's 2 (0,2,2,4) + ic4 (0,4); 0,2,6 = ic2 (0,2) + ic4 (2,6). Pc 10 completes 3-1 registrally and 4-1 contiguously. The jump to pc6 balances the opening ic9 by ic8. Placing these two ic's in the same register reveals that they extend the progression which resulted in the opening jump by ic1 and 2 (see above). The last pc's present 3-4 and 4-4, sets not previously found, but justifiable as being accidentally formed by the interlocking succession of 3-1 and the characteristic jump. (If pc11 is heard as being of very local level usage i.e., as an approach to pc10 – 3-3 is projected, comprised of pc's 9,[11],10,6.)

Stressed tones are pc8 (by virtue of register and length), pc10 (the result of local level motion by ic1 on either side), and pc6 (by register). These combine in 3-6. Compare the unfolding of intervals with the opening intervallic succession.

The second version of 6-Z3 begins on pc3, retained from its occurrence in the previous sonority. It proceeds to pc11 which combines with the following pc's 8,10 in 3-2 and 8,10,9 (3-1) in 4-1. The following pc6 completes 3-3 with pc's 10,9, as does pc5 with pc's 9,6. There are several difficulties here, however. First an apparent g# minor triad is formed by the first three pc's. Also, association by register and stress produces unjustified sets, as shown in example 137.

EX.137

3.5   3.4   4.27   (0,2,5,8)"B7"

The last version shown in example 135 re-works the same pitch content to better effect, and is the one included in example 133. First, pc3 is dispensed with and pc11 is placed in the lower octave to lie midway between pc's 8,3 of the previous sonority. If heard as progressing from pc3, the same apparent g# minor triad results. However, if pc11 is associated by instrumental color with pc7, a form of 3-3 will be projected as the link between the chordal and melodic statements. Again, the line opens with a leap of ic9, imitating the second ic of the opening sonority. The following pc10 completes 3-2 by way of the ascending ic2, the interval so prevalent in the previous chordal aggregate. The following pc9 completes 3-i, as did the opening progression of ic2 (pc's 0,2) and the succeeding pc1.

EX.138

The unprepared (contextually) ascending leap of the ending, also problematic in example 135 (pc's 8,9), is presented here between two different voices, just as in its previous chordal occurrence.

EX.139

This fragment, then, is a re-working and imitation of the first two intervals of the chord, which was, itself, a re-working of the original material.

EX.140

The separation of the last two pc's 5,6 in distinct voices prepares for a two-voice statement of intervallic succession, completing the presentation of materials as chord, melody, and finally as counterpoint.

EX.141

The opening ic1 progresses by oblique motion to ic2 and finally to ic4. The upper line progresses by ic1, the bottom by ic2, echoing the intervals formed by the preceding oblique motion. The entire collection forms 4-2, exposing subsets 3-1 (6,5,4), 3-3 (5,4,8), and 3-6 (6,8,4). The presentation of ic's 1 and 2 imitates 3-1 of the preceding melodic statement, both vertically and horizontally.

A new voice enters on pc10, extending the motion of ic2 (pc's 6,8) into another occurrence of 3-6, and combining vertically in 3-8, an extension of the linear set. This is followed by a melodic presentation of ic's 8,9.

Pc0, which begins the melodic statement, again extends the progression of ic2. Its downward jump to pc3 forms 3-3 in combination with the upper pc4. It then progresses to pc5 and reverses the jump to ic1, also forming 3-3 with the upper voice. This affects a connection of ic's 8,9 by ic2 below an ic1 above, again echoing earlier statements.

EX.142

The upper three voices next progress to a statement of 3-1 and finally 3-3. With pc1 below, the 4n sets are 4-4 (0,1,2,5) and 4-7 (0,1,4,5). The first is a combination of subsets 3-1 and 3-3, as occurred previously. The second is an expansion of 3-3.

EX.143

The voice-leading in the upper three voices is derived from the progression of ic's 8,9 as they occur in the lower voice and in the original material. Each progresses by a different interval; ic1 in the lowest voice, ic2 in the middle, and ic3 above. Pc8 in the upper voice completes 3-3 as a linear statement (pc's 5,4,8). The lowest voice combines in 3-2 (6,8,9). Pc's 3,5 in the lower voice connect registrally with pc11 which began the melodic statement, completing 3-8.

The following two-voice statement of ic's 2,8,2,8 is, of course, directly derived from the original materials, and is generated by pc1 of the melodic statement. Pc's 2,4 combine with pc1 to form 3-2, followed by 3-6 (pc's 3,11,1) and its extension 3-8 (7,9,1). This is, again, a recurrence of earlier materials. Pc's 2,4,3 are a reiteration of 3-1 as it originally occurred in the melodic line, and connects with the previous pc's 3,5 in the same register in 4-1, an extension of 3-1. The last pc8 of this progression occurs above to avoid accidental occurrence of the tonal set 0,3,7.

EX.144

The two-voice progression presents 3-1, 3-2, 3-3, 3-4, and 3-6.

EX.145

The exposed attack on ic8 acts to end the phrase begun on the contrapuntal statement and is followed by a rhythmic statement of chordal materials. This is prepared by pc6 (3-6, pc's 8,4,6) and pc3 (3-3, pc's 3,4,7). With the re-introduction of pc6, set 4-3 (0,1,3,4) is completed. The reiteration of pc's 7,6 is an occurrence of the rhythmic motive of the opening chordal aggregate and provides a quasi-melodic motion of ic1. The following addition of pc10 above and pc's 2,1 below forms 3-3, and extends 3-3 above (6,7,10). Pc2 combines in 3-1 with pc's 3,4. Its motion to pc1 forms 3-2 with the same lower two pc's of the held chord.

The next phrase repeats the rhythmically stated chord, which ends in a manner reminiscent of the opening chordal aggregate. Pc's 5,9 were chosen as they exist in the same register as the previous closely positioned chord, imparting a feeling of resolution to these tones. In combination with the previous upper voice pc10, newly added, 3-4 is formed. Both pc's 5,9 combine with the moving line consisting of pc's 2,1 in 3-3; 2,1,5 and 2,1,9. The following ic10, comprised of pc's 8,6, not only completes the large chromatic set begun in the rhythmically-stated chord, but each pc completes 3-3 with the held ic4, above (5,6,9 + 5,8,9 = 4-3). The opening phrase group is completed with the appearance of ic8 (pc's 7,3) which immediately elides into the next phrase. Relationships with the preceding 4-3 are shown in example 146.

EX.146

Notice the similarities in the opening and ending chordal aggregates.

EX.147

Also, pc6 plays a constant role, first introducing the initial contrapuntal statement, then in the rhythmically-stated chord, and finally in the reiteration of the chordal aggregate which ends the phrase-group. Ic4 (pc's 3,7), also recurs throughout in various registers, first in the chordal aggregate, then in the rhythmically-stated chord, and finally to end the phrase-group as the last and highest interval of the chord, preforming the same function by virtue of register and placement as in its original appearance. Combined with the recurrent pc6, an invariant 3-3 recurs throughout.

The next phrase-group begins, as did the first, with a melodic statement, this time occurring against the chordal aggregate instead of following. The similarity of chord and melody signals a significant structural moment.

The melody is comprised of the compliment of the six pc's of the chord, in an order suggested by a calculation of dissonance factors. Each pc of the complement was figured against the pc's of the chord and placed in a general order of decreasing dissonance. In the chart below, pc's of the chord are arrayed along the top, those of the melody to the left.

	Eb	F	F#	G	G#	A
C	3	1	4	1	2	3=14
Db	5	2	1	4	1	2=15
D	6	3	2	1	4	1=17
E	6	6	5	3	2	1=23
Bb	1	1	2	3	5	6=18
B	2	4	1	2	3	5=17

Their order was not accepted uncritically. Beginning on the most dissonant pc4, the next pc in order would be pc10, a distance of ic6 which has not figured prominently to this point. As there is little difference between a df of 17/6 or 18/6, we may choose to investigate the use of pc's 11,2 to follow pc4. While pc11 would result in another unused ic – 5 – pc2 would yield ic2, a very important interval. Either pc10 or pc11 could justifiably succeed pc2, but pc11 results in a new 3n set. Pc10 combines with pc's 4,2 in 3-8. The final ordering results in 3-8 (4,2,10), 3-3 (2,10,11), 3-2 (10,11,1) and 3-1 (11,1,0). The decreasing intervallic span of the sets imitates the importantly featured decreasing intervallic content of ic's 2,1, found throughout the preceding section, and as the last three pc's of the line.

Registral association also exposes prominent sets.

EX.148

Again, there is a conscious relation between this melodic statement and the first. Both present 3-2 followed by 3-1; pc's 11,8,10 and 8,10,9 echoed by 10,11,1 and 11,1,0. Just as the chordal aggregate was elided so the melodic statement is compressed.

Similarly, a contrapuntal statement follows, again beginning with oblique motion and involved in presenting 3-3. Here the set occurs in the lowest voice (pc's 1,0,9) and between the upper tones and the held pc0 (0,3,11). The upper line presents 4-11 (0,1,3,5), exposing subsets 3-6 (pc's 3,11,1) and 3-2 (pc's 11,1,10). The lower line is comprised of the other prominent sets; 3-3 (0,9,8), and 3-1 (9,8,7). Together they form the intervallic succession of ic's 4,2 (the intervals of sets 3-6 and 3-8), ending on ic3. This imitates the two-voice progression of ic2,8,2,8, heard previously.

EX.149

Sets formed are as follows:

EX.150

3.8   3.6   3.3   3.2   3.2

Both lines repeat the procedure of succession of decreasing intervals; ic's 4,(2),3 above and 3,1,1 below.

The following structures imitate not only the opening chordal aggregate but also the two-voice succession of ic's 2,4,2,4, and the second rhythmically stated chord. These pc's 2,5,4,6 form set 4-2, the complement of the eight pc's of the preceding two-voice statement.

EX.151

ic2, 3   ic2,4   ic4,3   ic3,2

The upper line progresses to ic8 (pc's 3,11) which is a retrograde of the original material. It is accompanied below by pc's 1,0 which, again, combine to form 4-2. Both four-voice vertical structures present 3-3 contiguously in the upper voices. The first shows 3-1 in the lower three, the second is 3-2. The last vertical sonority, 4-1, presents a progression of ic3(9) from every voice of the preceding 4n chord, arranged to present 3-1 in the upper voice and 3-2 in the lower. Other sets are shown in example 152.

EX.152

3.8   3.8   3.6   3.3   3.2   3.3   3.3   3.2   3.2

Pc8 is held to begin a short unaccompanied statement of ic8(4) and ic3, combining in 4-12 (0,2,3,6), a new 4n set. Its introduction here is justified by its ordering to present linking subsets 3-3 and 3-2 (8,0,11 and 0,11,2). A downward leap to pc6 completes the opening contour with ic8. The accompanying pc's 8,4 and 10,2 – both ic's 4 – are a chordal reiteration of the opening and closing ic's 4 of the melodic fragment. Both progress in each voice by ic2.

EX.153

The lower pc's present ic8, to answer the upward-moving ic's 9 of the previous bass register structures. It continues to pc's 0,4 (3-3), with pc4 linking in 3-3 with pc's 5,8. Pc7 completes 4-3 and 3-2 contiguously.

The ending sub-phrase of this group expands the number of voices employed, beginning on pc7. Set analysis is provided below.

EX.154

Obviously, some internally-occurring sets are not heard as strongly, and some other sets are clearly projected. What matters here is not only audibility and recognizable projection, but also progression and logical, justifiable generation.

The phrase group ends with the first complete statement of the generating material. It is expanded to include a lower voice, projecting 3-3 and an upper voice presenting ic3, linking at ic4 (intervals of 3-3) in 3-3 (pc's 7,10,6). Generating materials have already been examined. Three- and four-voice vertical collections are shown below.

EX.155

Notice the reflection of sets occurring horizontally and vertically in the original two-voice structure, formed by combination with newly added upper and lower lines.

As is amply evident, the procedures employed can be carried on indefinitely. The only limits are self-imposed constraints and imagination. It is quite a simple procedure to continue counterpoint and pitch generation, at will. However, it is meaningless unless guided by controlling factors in service to some structural, formal and procedural goals. Here, again, the only limitation is the strength with which your compositional logic and aims can be brought to bear.

compositional considerations

For the final project employing on-going variation, employ up to seven instruments (or more if a really complex and colorful work is within your abilities compositionally and instrumentally) drawn from strings and winds, with the inclusion of piano, if you wish. Any unfolding or succession of character, elements, procedures or instrumental colors may be employed. Give a dramatic shape to the overall structure. Be specifically aware of registral associations, especially in the outside line, and of the role which may be played by instrumental color in focusing lines and sets. Employ as great a variety and succession of textures as you can control. Use any and/or all procedures developed throughout this text as they become applicable or desirable to further your compositional aims. Remember to hear what you write and present it so that your communication to performer and listener is intelligible.

afterward

Not only this final piece, but your entire compositional career is limited only by your imagination, your mastery of craft and your skill in presenting your ideas. As you continue to write, each piece will inform and develop your abilities on all levels. You will begin to develop an arsenal of procedures, strictly your own, and a predilection for specific sonorities, sets, types of motion, instrumental usage, etc. These combine to form a style – your own particular voice. Follow your voice and your imagination, but be your own harshest critic.

The search for your style and voice is a long, often frustrating task. But it is the most fulfilling achievement in a composer's career. It makes the ultimate difference between composing unrelated exercises and functioning fully as a composer.

Made in the USA
Lexington, KY
01 September 2011